MANAGEMENT BASICS

Second Edition

A Practical Guide for Managers

Identify Strengths • Prioritize Objectives • Train Effectively • Control Finances • Resolve Differences

---

Sandra Gurvis

Technical Review by Barbara J. May,
Manager of Sales Operations, Qwest Communications

BUSINESS
Avon, Massachusetts

Published by Adams Business, an imprint of
Adams Media, an F+W Publications Company
57 Littlefield Street, Avon, MA 02322. U.S.A.
www.adamsmedia.com

ISBN-10: 1-59869-702-1
ISBN-13: 978-1-59869-702-5

Printed in the United States of America.

J I H G F E D C B

Library of Congress Cataloging-in-Publication Data
is available from the publisher.

*This book is available at quantity discounts for bulk purchases.
For information, please call 1-800-289-0963.*

Contents

CHAPTER 6 How to Make Decisions | 69

CHAPTER 7 Active Listening and Positive Persuasion | 81

CHAPTER 8 Teamwork and Coaching | 97

CHAPTER 9 How to Delegate | 115

CHAPTER 10 Presenting Information and Proposals | 127

Foreword

In the years since this book was first published, management has undergone huge and dramatic changes. Some have been for the better, but many present a double-edged sword.

The first and biggest upheaval has occurred within the workforce itself. Gone are the days when a Draconian manager with unhappy personnel was rewarded because the manager produced bottom-line results. Today's manager is more of a "collaborative coach" to a team of employees, whose input, if not required, is certainly at least encouraged. Although increasingly cross-functional teams are being used to solve many business problems, they suffer from frustratingly long decision-cycle times.

The workforce is far more diverse today than even a few years ago. Women, minorities, immigrants, foreign nationals, and others are not only a big part of this, but they have equal rights in the workplace. Rather than ignoring problems of sexual harassment and discrimination, most managers today work toward handling them fairly and equitably and listen to the viewpoints of all employees, no matter what their origin. And while federal regulations on family leave and individual religious beliefs in the workplace have encouraged a more balanced lifestyle for team members, they have added complexity to staffing and scheduling responsibilities for managers.

The workplace has also been revolutionized by corporate downsizing and outsourcing. Although both have done much to reduce the overall cost of doing business, many managers and employees have been left with huge workloads, not to mention the sense that their jobs may be declared "obsolete" (and eliminated) at any moment.

Other, equally major changes have taken place in technology—e-mail, the Internet, and accompanying devices that are supposed to make the workday easier, faster, and more efficient. Sometimes it has the opposite effect: While increasing the speed of communication, for example, e-mail has also resulted in unnecessary "clutter" of unimportant information. Managers must often sift through 200 to 300 e-mails a day to distill a few nuggets of important information. Instant communication devices such as the BlackBerry, cell phone, and pager make the manager more accessible but often turn her job into a 24/7, on-call proposition. The ubiquitous nature of the Internet provides customers easier access to information but presents challenges for managing the performance of employees who have online access during the workday.

Management has rarely been for the faint of heart. Given all of these stresses and expectations, it is even truer today. However, if you live by the maxim, "If you're not having fun it's your own darn fault," you can accept the responsibility for adjusting to these changes, make alterations in your management style, and help your staff move toward improved results and enhanced job satisfaction. This second edition of *Management Basics* offers helpful advice for navigating the transformed workscape and provides insight into how to adapt to—and dare we say, thrive with?—these and other changes that might come your way.

Barbara May, Chief of Staff
BMG Sales Operations-Credit, Collections,
Account Management, QCC Care and Order Processing
Qwest Communications International

INTRODUCTION

Using This Book

The first edition of *Management Basics* contained advice and straightforward explanations of what managers should and should not do. It also included such self-evaluation items as a questionnaire and worksheets. However, as Barbara May, who served as this book's technical advisor, noted in the preface, management has changed drastically since the first edition was first published in 1998. It has become much more complex and at times even apparently contradictory, a trend that's likely to continue as the world shrinks due to technology and the workplace becomes even more diverse and flexible in terms of not only the types of workers but the manner in which they do their jobs.

In response, and with Barbara's able advice and assistance, I have updated and expanded this edition, replacing the checklists and worksheets with information and suggestions from subject-matter experts (including, of course, John and Shirley Payne, the original authors). The focus is on providing a detailed overview for what can quickly become an overwhelming and all-encompassing task—even to those who have had previous management experience. Every company is different, with its particular way of doing things, so if you're starting in a new work situation, it's easy to ask, "Where the heck do I begin?" and "What have I gotten myself into?"

However, I also kept many of the basic concepts and tried to maintain the original authors' helpful, informative tone.

The chapters in this new edition are self-contained units that offer a logical progression in their approach to the essentials of management. Each chapter has a brief introduction and objectives, while takeaway points are summarized at the end. The book can be read in its entirety or you can select the chapters/areas of interest to you; the detailed Table of Contents and Index should be valuable in helping you locate specific topics.

Chapters 1 and 2 cover getting started—what is expected of a beginning manager and how the workforce has changed. Also discussed are working with telecommuters and "nontraditional" employees as well as various laws covered by the U.S. Equal Employment Opportunity Commission (EEOC), the Family Leave Act, and more.

Chapters 3 to 7 go back to the basics: goal setting, organizing your day and that of your team members, problem solving and decision-making, and how to listen and persuade. Now, more than ever managers must be attuned to what their employees are saying and doing and what is really going on (as opposed to what people might tell them!).

Chapter 8 stresses a relatively new concept to the business world—coaching—which has pretty much replaced counseling and "calling someone on the carpet" when managers want to improve performance. Similarly, Chapter 9 talks about delegation, especially important as managers are increasingly pressed for time to do more with less, while Chapters 10 and 11 offer guidance in another area where today's managers need to be well-versed: oral presentations, proposals, and handling the meeting. If you're a manager, chances are you'll be called to speak in front of a group, and how you present yourself in these situations can spell the difference between success and failure in reaching your various objectives.

Finally, Chapters 12 to 14 encompass performance—from motivating employees to managing appraisals to hiring and firing. As with mostly everything in today's workplace, certain procedures must be followed; the days of managing by the seat of one's pants (or through intimidation) are gone. Sensitivity tempered with logical decision-making is particularly vital in making decisions regarding team members, be it bringing them aboard, promoting them, or termination.

The original authors of *Management Basics* put forward a basic concept that permeates the book and still holds true: the application of the 80:20 rule. This rule says that you will often find an approximately 80:20 ratio between related factors; that is, that 80 percent of X (say, your work) derives from 20 percent of Y (for instance, your customers). With this in mind, you can begin to understand the importance of focusing on the 20 percent that needs to be attended to at any given moment. This provides a starting point in organizing your day and workload. So if you're in the thick of something and are not quite sure what to do, remember the 80:20 rule; it offers a good way to approach the solution.

As with most things, as you gain practice, you'll find management gets easier. I hope the advice and information found in this revised edition will aid in that process.

CHAPTER 1

You're a Manager — Now What?

CHAPTER OBJECTIVES

To define management

To help you make the transition from worker to manager

To give an overview of what's expected of you as a manager

To provide information on what's needed of an effective manager

To help you begin to develop your management style

INTRODUCTION

Congratulations are in order if you're a new manager or even if you've had management experience and are looking for a refresher course. Sometimes it's good to sit back and take a look at the "big picture" of management.

The purpose of this chapter is to provide an introduction to and brief overview of management. Who manages, and why? What are the defined methods of management and how can you apply them to your day-to-day operations? Sometimes the most basic concepts can provide answers in ways you might not expect.

One of the most important things that all managers—beginning and otherwise—need to understand is their corporate culture and mission. Once you are clear on those, then you can begin to develop a plan of action and goals, which will be discussed in further chapters.

WHAT IS A MANAGER?

Look up the word *manager* on the Internet or in any reference book and you will find many different definitions. They range from the coach of a sporting team to an individual hired to manage a celebrity's business or personal affairs to a server that provides the communication link between the systems administrator and affiliated devices on a computer network. But the most common definition is of someone responsible for directing or organizing a group of employees or a project. In other words, someone like you.

Managers of various organizations and companies come in many "flavors"—they can be directors, group or section leaders, various vice presidents, chief operating officers, even heads of boards of directors. In the truest sense, even the president of the United States is a manager.

According to management expert Bill Warner,[1] all managers have several things in common, despite their varying responsibilities: They are leaders, project managers, and coaches who use department resources—both people and equipment—to get the job done. They develop strategies, organize the department, set priorities and make decisions, place and ensure the training of their workers, delegate responsibilities, find solutions, make sure employees have adequate resources to do the job, communicate with department and outside sources, and represent and help determine company policy.

Managers also have a number of "soft" duties: establishing and solidifying relationships within and outside of the company; creating and nurturing a positive work environment so people can support each other within the team; and coaching—working with individuals to improve their performance so they have a clear idea of how they can contribute and thus put forward their best efforts. Managers also serve as mentors, encouraging new talent and advising their employees on their career path, as well as acting as a conduit to higher-level management on the progress of their department and other issues that can affect corporate decision-making.

When it comes down to it, managers are responsible for everything in their arena. No matter what or how many people you manage, when it comes to your area of responsibility, the buck stops with you.

THE FUNCTION OF MANAGEMENT: THE 80:20 RULE

Vast amounts of information exist outlining what a manager should and should not do. In fact, there is so much information it is very difficult for someone who wants to learn to know where to start. And even when you know where to look, no one can learn everything. The principal objective must therefore be to identify those ideas that will produce the bulk of the results—and that is an application of the 80:20 rule.

If you don't already know this rule, it states that you will often find an (approximately) 80:20 ratio between related factors. For example:

80 PERCENT	80 PERCENT	80 PERCENT
of the sales revenue derives from	*of the problems are caused by*	*of the results come from*
20 PERCENT	20 PERCENT	20 PERCENT
of the customers	*of the people*	*of the activities*

With this in mind, you can begin to understand the importance of focusing on the 20 percent that needs to be attended to at any given moment. Focusing on the 20 percent allows managers to prioritize how they spend their time. Because they often lack experience, new managers will find that their schedule fills up quickly—they can't do everything. Prioritizing enables the manager to have an impact without spending sixty hours a week in the office.

The 80:20 rule enables you to weed out the problems and concentrate on the areas needing improvement. It will also help you identify strengths within your organization, as well as benchmark high achievers.

FROM "BEING MANAGED" TO MANAGER

In a sense, becoming a manager is like having a child. Before your promotion, you were only responsible for one person: yourself. Now you've got other people to look out for: your employees and team members. The decisions you make will affect them—and their careers—as well.

So how do you make the transition from a good worker who produced solid results—resulting in your promotion—to managing others and achieving the same (or greater) level of success?

The first step is *managing yourself.* This includes obvious areas like staying in shape, eating and sleeping well; being accountable for your actions; doing your best; being a good listener; and other concepts discussed in this book. As a manager, you'll be leading by example, and it will set the tone for your entire department. Your responsibilities are to motivate your team members to do the best work possible and shaping the team into a cohesive unit that gets the job done.

So you'll want to set a standard for personal excellence, whether it be through taking additional training (and encouraging your team to do so); learning new skills, such as public speaking (even if you have stage fright); and being positive. The latter is especially important in obtaining cooperation from employees, who must feel that you are loyal and they can trust you. They also need to be comfortable coming to you with their ideas as well as having the sense that you will act upon their feedback and suggestions.

Employees will do their best when working for someone who they believe in and can turn to. They also expect you to be more than competent, if not on the cutting edge of your area of expertise. That said, you also need to recognize your weaknesses and theirs, as well as defining areas of improvement and growth.

UNDERSTANDING THE CORPORATE CULTURE

Corporate culture is often defined as "how we do things around here" and reflects the organization's personality, attitudes, experiences, beliefs, and values. A company is like a living, breathing organism, as individual as a snowflake.

Simple things can often trip up a new manager who is not "schooled" in the cultural norms of the organization. Who to copy or not to copy on e-mail, when and if to skip links in the chain of command, how to act when you are directly engaged by your boss's boss, the tone to take in written communications and meetings (direct versus political), how to act at social functions (to drink or not to drink, who to sit with, etc.) are just a few areas the new manager must be cognizant of.

Theories abound that explain corporate culture. Among the most insightful and commonly used is a model from MIT professor Ed Schein[2] who describes it as existing on three cognitive levels. At the first or "surface" level are the attributes that can be seen by the outside observer—physical layout, dress code, how employees interact with each other, the company's policies and procedures, and organizational structure. The next "middle" level consists of the professed culture of the company: its mission statements, slogans, and stated values. At the third and deepest level are the organization's tacit assumptions, the "unspoken rules" rarely consciously acknowledged even by the employees. Here you'll find taboo and sometimes contradictory elements of company culture.

It is in this last area that managers face their greatest challenge. Not only do they need to understand all three levels, but they must also know how to navigate the complex and often conflicting third level, a task that requires the utmost tact and sensitivity. To ignore or bypass the company's unspoken rules and taboos is to invite trouble and resistance among the ranks and from other managers. The best way to prevent inadvertent slip-ups is to find a peer or manager who can help you understand the more subtle nuances of accepted practices. It also helps to be observant and especially at first to listen, more than offering opinions.

It's also useful to understand which type of corporate culture you're dealing with. Deal and Kennedy[3] describe four different kinds of culture:

- Work-hard, play-hard culture (*rapid feedback/reward and low risk—restaurants and software companies*)
- Tough-guy macho culture (*rapid feedback/reward and high risk—police, surgeons, sports*)

- Process culture (*slow feedback/reward and low risk—banks, insurance companies*)
- Bet-the-company culture (*slow feedback/reward and high risk—aircraft manufacturers, Internet ventures*)

As a manager, you should wholeheartedly support your company's culture, even if you don't agree with parts of it. Change is more easily effected if it's perceived as friendly and coming from within the organization, rather than from an external, potentially hostile force, such as a corporate takeover or outside consultant.

DEFINING YOUR ROLE—GET CLEAR ON WHAT YOU NEED TO DO

Unlike its culture, a company's mission statement is clear-cut. It conveys to the world what the company is about and what it hopes to accomplish. As a manager, you may want to create your own mission statement, even if it's concerning a project or department that you've inherited from someone else. If it's a new venture, then you're faced with the challenge of coming up with something from scratch. First and foremost the mission statement for your organization should reflect and reinforce the mission of the company. Either way, you might want to work in conjunction with your staff or team to develop the statement so it reflects the group's ideals.

An effective mission statement should cover the following:

- The department's purpose and objectives
- Its basic philosophy
- How it plans to serve customers, and the community at large
- The department's standards
- How the department will make a difference and fit into the overall scheme of things

Keep in mind that writing an effective mission statement is easier said than done.

It should summarize principles and ideals in only a few sentences as in the following example.

OHIO STATE UNIVERSITY MEDICAL CENTER'S MISSION, VISION AND VALUES

All areas of our organization are driven by our mission: to improve people's lives through innovation in research, education and patient care.

We also share a common vision: working as a team, we will shape the future of medicine by creating, disseminating and applying new knowledge, and by personalizing health care to meet the needs of each individual.

Central to how we carry out our mission and vision are our values: integrity, teamwork, innovation, excellence and leadership.

Source: Ohio State University Medical Center © 2007. Used with permission of Ohio State University Medical Center.

A solid, well-crafted mission statement will help you get clear on your goals as a manager and set forth the department's reason for existence as well as its objectives.

SETTING UP YOUR MANAGEMENT STYLE

The $100,000 (adjusted for inflation) question facing many beginning managers is: How should I lead? To begin to answer that question, it's helpful to have a grasp of the most common management styles:

- An *autocratic manager* makes all the decisions, keeping the information and decision-making among the senior management.
- A *paternalistic manager* makes decisions in an authoritarian manner in what he perceives is in the best interests of the employees.

- A *democratic manager* allows the employees to participate in decision-making; everything is determined by the majority.
- A *laissez-faire manager* takes a peripheral role, allowing staff members to manage their own arenas of responsibility.

None of these styles is the "right" one. Managers can use any or all of them. You may be more comfortable with one style, or more commonly, a combination of styles, depending upon the corporate culture or what the situation warrants.

It's also important to understand what drives your employees. Decades ago, the role of management was perceived as almost punitive, "making" employees do things because they were believed to be inherently lazy and only out for the paycheck. This "old school" of thought, known as *Theory X management,* was developed by the late Douglas McGregor,[4] a management professor at MIT. According to Theory X, employees are like unruly children, needing close supervision. The manager assigns blame when things go wrong.

McGregor also developed *Theory Y management* to cover the other end of the spectrum. According to this theory, employees see work as a natural part of their lives. Not only will they accept responsibility but they actually embrace their physical and mental duties. Therefore, employees should be given total freedom to perform at the best of their abilities without restrictions or punishment.

Taken at either extreme, both theories have their problems. With Theory X, you have management by fear and intimidation, which is ineffective in eliciting loyalty and long-term results. This style of management limits idea generation since the manager assumes he has all the answers and that those answers are always right and best. Theory Y may cause a breakdown in communication because managers hesitate to interfere or hurt employees' feelings. Human nature being what it is, employees may take advantage of Theory Y managers.

Obviously the best approach is somewhere in the middle, a combination of "tough" and "tender." In real life—as in the workplace—most situations fall somewhere in between, with an occasional need to go to either extreme. However, these models remain useful in figuring out effective approaches to management and organizational development issues.

TIPS AND TRAPS FOR BEGINNING MANAGERS

One of my favorite sayings is, "If it was easy, everyone could do it!" Management expert Robert Crittendon[5] cites a Code of Conduct for beginning managers, which can apply to all managers, regardless of their level or experience.

- Don't say things about someone behind his back that you wouldn't say to his face.
- Maintain absolute integrity in all things at all time.
- Praise in public, criticize in private.
- Treat your word as your bond, and keep every promise you make.
- Accept responsibility for your actions.
- Accept the fact that success is not final and failure is not fatal.
- Don't be afraid of making a mistake, but never repeat the same mistakes.
- If you need professional advice get it from professionals, not from friends.

Crittendon also emphasizes the importance of focusing on doing things right, even down to the smallest detail (consider the consequences of an erroneous prescription or mistakes in accounting, for example); becoming a good personal communicator; and not taking yourself too seriously.

It goes back to managing yourself, mentioned on page 6. Being able to keep things in perspective and taking time for yourself, as well as your hobbies and family, will give you a sense of balance and enable you to make well-thought-out decisions. Workaholics fall into the trap of becoming one-dimensional and believing they're indispensable. Consider this: A hundred years from now, is anyone going to care whether you stayed at the office until 10 P.M.? (They might, however, care what your children or grandchildren are like or if you've done something to make the world a better place.) You'll produce better results—and get more from your team—if you focus on the outcomes rather than the number of hours spent at a desk or in meetings.

TAKE-AWAY POINTS

- Managers are responsible for the "hard" duties—organizing resources and making decisions—and the "soft" duties of networking and providing support. Both are equally important in getting the job done.
- Eighty percent of the results come from 20 percent of the activities. So focus on the 20 percent of tasks that need to be done.
- The most effective managers take care of themselves both physically and mentally and live balanced lives. They lead by example and set high standards for personal excellence.
- Understanding more than just the surface traits of your corporate culture, including its unspoken rules and seeming contradictions, will help you make in-depth and effective decisions.
- As a manager, you need to wholeheartedly support your corporate culture and mission statement. With the help of your team, you can craft your own mission statement to help get clear on your goals.
- There are a variety of management styles, but rather than focusing on a specific one, pay attention to what the situation seems to warrant. Some may require strict supervision, while others necessitate a take-charge attitude. Still others are best served by a laissez-faire management style.
- Personal accountability is the single most important trait of a manager. Being approachable, flexible, and results-oriented are also vital.

CHAPTER 2

New Rules for Management

CHAPTER OBJECTIVES

To provide an overview of current trends in management

To introduce you to the legal ramifications involving supervision

To provide guidance in working with telecommuters, knowledge workers, and creative people

To help you manage in an increasingly diverse environment

To further define your role in an ever-evolving workplace

INTRODUCTION

The management landscape has changed dramatically over the past several years, and thanks to technology, a knowledge-based economy, and the need to cut costs, it will continue to evolve. The workplace is also far more diverse, not only in terms of race and nationality but also in dealing with a worldwide economy. The days of managing by the seat of your pants are gone forever, and you must be familiar with everything from labor laws to immigration regulations to the rights of union workers. At the very least, managers need to know how to obtain accurate information to deal with these and other issues.

Managers will also likely be working with "alternative" employees—telecommuters and independent contractors. These—and in fact all employees—must be treated equitably regardless of age, race, creed, or physical ability.

HOW THE WORKFORCE HAS CHANGED

Change is a constant in today's workplace. Gone is the era of gold watches and golden parachutes; even government workers no longer have the long-term job security they once had. Technology has certainly played a huge part in this, first with computers, then e-mail and instant messaging. Next came cell phones and text messaging, high-speed Internet and Ethernets, wireless platforms, and downloading capabilities for music and video. Just as George Orwell predicted in *1984*, surveillance cameras are everywhere—at the bank, the grocery store, and in the elevator. Using such Internet services as Google Earth you can watch the movements of any given location on the planet 24/7. The days of Xeroxing your hand (or any other anatomical part) and passing it around as an anonymous office joke are gone forever (most copiers have a function that identifies users).

The office landscape has dramatically altered as well. We started with casual Fridays, and now often have casual workweeks; flex-time and then telecommuting. Offices emphasize team-building rather than an organizational chart or hierarchy, and implement continuous process improvement programs such as Six Sigma. These are but a few of the recent and often overwhelming developments that have been assimilated into managerial culture.

It's natural that employees themselves have been deeply affected by these changes. Where once workers had their arenas of responsibility and were specialized—they knew what was expected of them and when—the knowledge-based economy influenced by many of the above-mentioned changes has demanded that they be more flexible. Factors affecting their jobs and the way they do them include outsourcing—using vendors or outside contracts to reduce overall labor costs—downsizing, unexpected switching or adding of job duties, and corporate takeovers and mergers.

According to the Department of Labor, workers from ages eighteen to thirty-eight change jobs an average of ten times. In fact most people switch careers three to seven times in their lifetimes. Most workers recognize the tentativeness of their positions, as management constantly restructures to save money or increase productivity or their companies are bought or sold by outside interests.

How to Deal with Change

Today's managers need be sensitive to the changing workplace. Motivational speaker and author Ida Covi[6] recommends the following:

Prepare managers. It's the trickle-down effect: Top leadership needs to inform all levels of management what's happening. Companies should train managers in how to deal with change so they can handle it properly.

Communicate early and often. Everyone should be kept up-to-date on the latest decisions, even if it doesn't directly affect employees. This is the reverse of the traditional "need to know." However, it will help employees feel like a part of the process, and in fact may deepen their commitment to the company.

Acknowledge emotions. Any kind of change is usually difficult, so workers should be assured that management cares about them and will do everything it can to help.

Increase "emotional intelligence" companywide. Employees also need to acknowledge their own feelings so they can deal with them. Open discussion, as well as positive suggestions for handling anger and stress in a productive manner, should be encouraged.

Additionally, in designing how the work is done a new manager should solicit the aid and opinions of those whom they manage. Not only will this produce a more effective process, but when the staff knows they have an element of control it will enhance their buy-in to the changes.

Perhaps most importantly, and especially during periods of change, at all times managers should be honest. Even if you aren't at liberty to divulge certain details of high-level decisions in the company, it's better to say you can't talk about it than be evasive and lie. In the final analysis, all you have is your credibility, and once that's compromised it will be difficult to regain employees' trust.

LABOR LAWS

Everyone jokes about political correctness, but the reality is that the workplace can be a veritable time bomb of litigation. Although many of the laws have been around for decades, some are more recent. Their effects are long reaching.

The federal laws prohibiting job discrimination are:

- Title VII of the Civil Rights Act of 1964, which prohibits employment discrimination based on race, color, religion, sex, or national origin
- The Equal Pay Act of 1963 (EPA), which protects men and women who perform substantially equal work in the same establishment from sex-based wage discrimination
- The Age Discrimination in Employment Act of 1967 (ADEA), which protects individuals who are forty years of age or older
- Title I and Title V of the Americans with Disabilities Act of 1990 (ADA), which prohibit employment discrimination against qualified individuals with disabilities in the private sector and in state and local governments
- Sections 501 and 505 of the Rehabilitation Act of 1973, which prohibit discrimination against qualified individuals with disabilities who work in the federal government
- The Civil Rights Act of 1991, which, among other things, provides monetary damages in cases of intentional employment discrimination

The U.S. Equal Employment Opportunity Commission (EEOC) enforces all of these laws. The EEOC also provides oversight and coordination of all federal equal employment opportunity regulations, practices, and policies.

Another federal law, the Family and Medical Leave Act of 1993 (FMLA), allows any eligible employee to take up to twelve workweeks of unpaid leave during any twelve-month period to care for a newborn child, for seriously ill family members, or if they themselves develop a serious health condition, among other contingencies. (For more information, see *http://www.dol.gov/esa/whd/ fmla.*)

Each state has its own laws against discrimination in addition to enforcement agencies. Although there are few laws preventing discrimination on the basis of sexual orientation (gays, transgender), managers should be sensitive to this area as well. Given the recent controversy about same-sex marriage, it follows that the rights of gays will be eventually addressed in the workplace. The cold reality is that many of these issues—particularly relating to age and sex—come into play more often then they should in decisions regarding hiring and promotion.

To protect themselves legally, managers should avoid knowing the employee's age, sexual orientation, or family situation. Although this may seem somewhat stringent, consider that upon legal review, you as manager may be perceived as having used this information to make decisions about which employee to promote, terminate, and so forth.

Managers who are conversant with state and federal equal labor laws, who are more interested in results, solid teamwork, and looking for the best person for the job, and who treat all team members with professionalism and respect run much less risk of encountering complaints of discrimination. Information about equal labor laws can be found at *www.eeoc.gov*; most states also have a specific Web site for their laws.

MULTICULTURAL MANAGEMENT

The world is shrinking in more ways than one. The increased emphasis on a global economy has forced companies to develop programs and procedures to deal with different cultures. Giant conglomerates such as Pepsi are tapping into specialized ethnic markets by producing such items as guacamole-flavored Doritos for Hispanics, Mountain Dew Code Red for African Americans, and a wasabi-flavored snack aimed at Asians.

So whether your team members come from a foreign country and/or speak a different language, or you're working with other cultures virtually from behind your desk—an increasingly common occurrence—or visiting overseas sites, you'll be faced with greater challenges than just learning how to communicate with them verbally. Not only are there vast differences in how things get done, but when it comes to business many countries outside of the United States are much more relationship-oriented. They'll select the company they know and trust, even if it charges twice as much as an unknown company.

Author and business consultant Paul Tulenko[7] suggests the following steps in making the most out of a multicultural workforce:

1. **Identify the diversity.** Find out about the various cultures represented by your workforce. Each has a different way of processing information and dealing with situations.
2. **Discover the norms.** Find out everything you can about their culture—from books, from others who have lived and worked in the culture, and perhaps most importantly from the employees themselves.
3. **Discern the differences.** As mentioned earlier, each culture does things its own way. What may be acceptable in one is completely offensive in another. If you get an inkling that you might have done something wrong or unacceptable in your dealings with a worker from another culture, find a trusted expert and discuss the situation (in some cultures, direct questions in themselves are considered offensive).
4. **Recognize the necessity.** There is no "textbook" way of dealing with different cultures. The most effective way to understand a culture is to spend time in the country yourself. If that's physically impossible, hire or consult with those who have expertise in multicultural relationships.

Religiously diverse workforces also present challenges. Observance of holidays and the Sabbath can have an impact on work hours and overtime. Managers must also be sensitive to implications regarding customs of dress when employees are in customer-facing roles. It's vitally important to understand multicultural implications and nuances both within your team and as it relates to your business. Culture change agents and even courses in multiculturalism can help bridge the gap.

TELECOMMUTING AND VIRTUAL MANAGEMENT

According to the U.S. Department of Labor approximately one in ten employees has an "alternative work arrangement." This category encompasses independent contractors, on-call workers, and temporary employees—in essence, anyone outside the traditional 9-to-5 office environment. Another rapidly growing classification is full-time employees who physically work in another location and are supervised "from a distance."

You may find yourself managing one or more of these types of individuals. So how do you get the job done and maintain a cohesive team without engendering resentment from "regular" staff members?

- Recognize that most telecommuters are highly motivated. Although managers may fear that the lack of face-to-face, daily contact will result in lowered productivity, the opposite is often true. Successful telecommuters are results-oriented. If they don't get the work done, they don't have a job. They know they can be easily replaced.
- Schedule regular meetings or conference calls that involve the entire team, including telecommuters and on-site workers. This way, they'll get to know each other and develop a working relationship, even if only virtually. Invite telecommuters to special events, such as dinners and company get-togethers.
- Be specific as to what you expect from a telecommuter/virtual worker. Since she's not in the office on a daily basis, she's likely unacquainted with the nuances of office politics. Make sure she knows what to do and when it's expected.

- Respect office hours. Just because someone "works from home" doesn't give you the right to call him at 10 p.m. or on weekends. Conversely, telecommuters should be available to you during working hours. Make sure you're accessible as well. If not, delegate that responsibility to someone who can provide needed answers and advice.
- Offer recognition and praise. Because they lack face-to-face contact, virtual employees may feel their efforts fall between the cracks or are neglected and ignored. Providing rewards—whether it's a plaque, recognition within the department, or a bonus—will raise their profile among the rest of the team as well as enhance their sense of being a valued part of the organization.

The beauty of virtual workers/telecommuters is that it can be a a "win-win" for everyone. The employee can set their own schedule and spend more time with family, and the manger can get quality work while saving money on overhead. In order for the situation to work, however, there must be give-and-take between both parties and a sense of commitment toward getting the job done.

CREATIVE PEOPLE AND KNOWLEDGE WORKERS

The shift to a knowledge-based economy (as opposed to an industrial or service-based one) has resulted in an explosion of workers who not only create information but disseminate it. These people are known as *creatives* and *knowledge workers*. Creatives consist of artists, writers, musicians, videographers, and anyone who generates new material in a variety of art forms. Knowledge workers deal primarily with information, using and disseminating it in the workplace. This category of workers also includes those in the information technology fields (systems analysts, programmers, technical writers, academics, researchers) as well as more general disciplines like teachers, scientists, and lawyers.

Although they can do vastly different kinds of work, creatives and knowledge workers can be managed in a similar manner. This is because they are primarily *self-motivated*. If you try to micromanage or closely supervise them, demanding constant reports on their progress, you'll likely encounter resistance and lowered productivity, in addition to creating an unnecessarily stressful workplace that hampers ideas and problem solving.

Following are some additional tips for managing creatives and knowledge workers:[8]

- Cultivate a space conducive to their work habits. Where do they seem most productive: on their own or as part of a group? Ask for their opinions, and if possible allow them input as to how and where they will work.
- Along with freedom, provide some structure. Creative people in particular tend to be flighty, so offer general guidance as to deadlines and schedules. Gently remind them when "boring" routine work such as reports and other paperwork is due.
- Understand that creatives and knowledge people need "thinking time." They may not look like they're doing much, but they're actually processing information and figuring out designs in their heads. As long as they meet deadlines and do their work correctly, don't sweat the small stuff if they're not chained to their desks the full eight hours. You should provide opportunities for them to periodically update you on the status during the course of a project or piece of work.
- On the other hand, provide them with full knowledge of the "big picture." Creatives and knowledge workers can get off-track and hung up on smaller details. But if you give them a complete view of the problem or issue, they can come up with surprising and innovative solutions.
- Remember to provide recognition and praise. Although it may seem as if the work itself is its own reward, if they don't feel as if they're in an integral part of the team, they may go elsewhere. And if they're really good, they'll easily find another job.

AVOIDING LEGAL COMPLICATIONS

Earlier in this chapter, we discussed labor laws—men and women must be paid equitably, and you cannot discriminate on the basis of age, race, sex, disability, or religious preference, among other things. These issues seem to come up particularly when hiring or firing, so managers should be conversant with the kinds of questions to ask when hiring. Fully document any reasons for firing an employee, closely following procedures set forth by company policy and labor laws.

For instance, you can't inquire during a job interview whether someone has been arrested. They are only required to disclose this information if they have been convicted of a felony (and even then, the felony must be directly related to the duties of the position for you to use it as an acceptable reason to disqualify the individual).

Some other potential legal trips and traps include the following.

Sexual Harassment

There have been many landmark court cases regarding this, and they have established that the burden of proof is on the employer. If you or your company has been accused of sexual harassment, it's up to you to prove your innocence. As with many things, the best medicine is prevention. Have a well-publicized company policy prohibiting sexual harassment, and make it easy for complainants to contact management regarding these matters. Also make sure to investigate all complaints, no matter how seemingly unfounded, keep thorough records, and follow through to their resolution.

The EEOC defines sexual harassment as "unwelcome sexual advances, requests for sexual favors, and other verbal or physical conduct of a sexual nature . . . when this conduct explicitly or implicitly affects an individual's employment, unreasonably interferes with an individual's work performance, or creates an intimidating, hostile, or offensive work environment."

Sexual harassment can occur in a variety of circumstances, including but not limited to the following:

- The victim as well as the harasser may be a woman or a man. The two parties do not have to be of the opposite sex.
- The harasser can be the victim's supervisor, an agent of the employer, a supervisor in another area, a coworker, or a nonemployee.
- The victim does not have to be the person harassed but could be anyone affected by the offensive conduct.
- Unlawful sexual harassment may occur without economic injury to or discharge of the victim.
- The harasser's conduct must be unwelcome. (Source: *www.eeoc.gov/types/sexual_harassment.html.*)

Most states also have laws against sexual harassment. Interestingly enough, in 2006, of the more than 12,000 charges of sexual harassment filed with the EEOC, more than 15 percent were from males!

To protect the accuser and accused, the manager should treat any case of sexual harassment as confidential, involving only those within the company on a "need to know" basis.

Foreign Nationals

Volatile and rapidly changing, immigration law represents a complicated regulatory mishmash best left to legal experts. Suffice to say, should you hire a foreign national (the government still uses that unfriendly and *Star Trek*–esque term *aliens*), make sure they have their "green card" and/or other permits to work. At minimum, this includes examination of identification documents and requiring the applicant to complete Form I-9. Although it may seem easiest to avoid hiring noncitizens altogether, keep in mind that it's considered discrimination if you *don't* hire someone because of his or her nationality. The only reason not to hire the foreign national over the citizen is if the citizen is better qualified for the job.

Foreign nationals can greatly enhance your team, particularly when you're recruiting for hard-to-fill jobs such as nurses, engineers, and technicians. Often exchange students who are learning a field related to your work goals can become valued team members. Regardless of whom you hire or for what type of position, check with the U.S. Citizenship and Immigration Services (USCIS, *www.uscis.gov*) regarding particular information on forms, regulations, and processing of permits. Remember that hiring undocumented foreign nationals is considered a felony in some cases and can result in fines, imprisonment, or forfeiture of property. So proceed with care!

Unions

While some may think labor unions have gone the route of Jimmy Hoffa, such is not the case; laws have been in place protecting unions since the 1930s—the Wagner Act (1935) is the most important of these laws. When you hire someone, you can't inquire if he is a member of a union, nor can you discriminate against someone if he is in a union. However, some states have passed "right to work" laws that prohibit a company or union from requiring membership in that union as a condition of employment. (Some companies are considered "closed" shops—they can only hire members of the union with which they have contracts. "Union shops" can hire nonunion members, but they must join the union.)

As you can see, it gets complicated pretty quickly, especially when a union tries to establish itself in a company whose management does not welcome its presence. As with any matter regarding unions, consult a lawyer who specializes in labor relations.

Managing in a union environment presents huge challenges, especially in regards to taking disciplinary actions against a unionized employee. The new manager should consult an HR specialist within his company for guidance as to what actions to take and be prepared for possible actions from the union.

Workers Compensation

The Cornell University Law School offers this explanation of Workers Compensation:

> *Workers Compensation laws are designed to ensure that employees who are injured or disabled on the job are provided with fixed monetary awards, eliminating the need for litigation. The laws also provide benefits for dependents of workers killed because of work-related accidents or illnesses. Some laws also protect employers and fellow workers by limiting the amount an injured employee can recover from an employer and by eliminating the liability of coworkers in most accidents.*
>
> *State Workers Compensation statutes establish this framework for most employment. Federal statutes are limited to Federal employees or those workers employed in some significant aspect of interstate commerce.*
>
> *Most workers compensation laws limit awards to "disability or death" sustained while in the performance of duties but not caused willfully by the employee or by intoxication. They cover medical expenses due to the disability and may require the employee to undergo job retraining. A disabled employee receives a percentage of their normal salary during the disability and may receive more for permanent physical injuries, or if he or she has dependents.*[9]

TAKE-AWAY POINTS

- This isn't your grandfather's—or even your mother's—workplace. Technology, a more flexible work environment, and a team-oriented approach have dramatically altered the landscape. Employees sense that times are uncertain as well, so be upfront and prepared to deal with the ramifications of change.

- Although the Equal Employment Opportunity Commission (EEOC) administers a variety of labor laws, you'll need to consider other factors such as state laws, the rights of individuals (such as gays and foreign nationals), and the reality that discrimination still exists in the workplace. You can do your part by being fair and treating all team members with professionalism and respect.

- Management is liable for sexual discrimination and harassment, workers compensation, immigration law, and more. Learn as much as you can, and make sure you have the resources to obtain advice and guidance in these areas.

- A growing global economy has resulted in two major trends—an increasingly multicultural workforce and a need to understand and interact with cultures of other countries. Managers who fail to recognize this may find themselves at a great disadvantage, and their companies may suffer as well.

- Also increasingly common are "alternative" employees—knowledge workers, creatives, and telecommuters. Make sure you're aware of their special requirements and needs as more and more companies downsize and use this resource.

CHAPTER 3

Goal Setting and Achievement

CHAPTER OBJECTIVES

To provide a working definition of goal setting and planning

To describe how goal setting and planning are important and interlinked

To provide principles that will help you to set goals for yourself and others and to plan

INTRODUCTION

To be an effective manager, you need to achieve results. In order to do that, you must first clearly define those results then decide how you are going to accomplish them. That means setting goals and planning.

WHAT IS GOAL SETTING?

Goal setting means identifying and defining the specific results required. Goals are important—unless you know where you are going, you may end up someplace you'd rather not be or someplace other than where you want to go. Have you ever been given a vague "goal" and been told later that you didn't do what was required? Such an experience was undoubtedly frustrating for everyone involved.

The ability to establish and define effective results-oriented goals is central to good management and should underlie everything you, as a manager, do. The most successful managers know where they are going, even though they may at times be unsure as to the best way to get there. They decide what the future should look like and work with their team to make that vision a reality.

It is also important to separate goals from aims. An *aim* is a general intention and is not as specific as a goal or objective. For example, a production manager might have the aim of "improving the quality of widgets produced as the reject rate is too high." That is an intention. A goal or objective, however, might be, say, "to reduce the reject rate on widgets from 6 percent to 3 percent within six months without recruiting additional inspection staff." The aim has now been turned into a specific result that can be achieved through various means.

Planning and Why It Is Important

The goal sets out where we are going, while the plan defines how we are going to get there. One approach is to say, "We have our goal, so let's just get on with it." But that can easily result in duplication of effort or in an important task being missed because everybody thought someone else was doing it. You need to plan. A plan subdivides the work and ensures that resources are used effectively.

DECIDE ON YOUR GOALS

A question managers new to the job sometimes ask is, "I know that I need to get results, but where do I start?" Office managers send invoices out on time, and production managers must move finished products out of the door. But of course there's more to it than that. So in addition to the primary purpose of the department, examine a few indicators to help decide where results are required.

Start by asking yourself, "What am I here for?" and jot down your thoughts on paper. At this stage just your initial ideas will be sufficient. Then look at the following list of "key results areas" and decide where you'd like to achieve results. There are examples for each area. Some may relate to your goals, or you might think of others. Make sure to focus on results rather than on activities.

You might also want to consider using what's known as the theory of the Golden Thread. This is a belief that a manager's goals should be derived from the goals of their superiors. The superiors' goals are derived from the goals of their superiors, and so forth, thus following the "golden thread" to the top of the hierarchy.

DETERMINING DESIRED RESULTS	
KEY RESULTS AREAS	*EXAMPLES*
Primary role	Meet/exceed sales revenue targets
Productivity	Delivery times could be reduced
Quality	Fewer errors on invoices
People	Reduce lateness
Finance	Travel costs are high
Administration	Some reports are not needed
Training and development	Develop Ken into assistant role
New ideas	Scrap useless procedures
Customers	Find out how they see us
Special projects	Set up information database

KEEP THEM SIMPLE AND FOCUSED

The table above focuses on specific activities rather than the "big picture." This is the most important aspect of goalsetting—breaking it into small, manageable pieces. For example, if sales in your department are down 25 percent and you look at it all at once, you might think, "That's terrible! How can we pull ourselves out of this tailspin?"

However, when you examine each aspect of the problem, patterns begin to emerge. In researching the product you might find that the sales force isn't up to date on the latest information. From that you could set a goal to make sure they're trained in the newest technology.

Or you may find that the sales team is lacking on the number of calls they're making. Set a goal for them of X number of calls per week. Finally, you might see that you've lost several key customers. Your new goal would be to revisit those customers and try to find out what went wrong, understand their needs, and see if they have been met or just not understood. Now you've got a clear idea of what caused the drop in sales. Additional goals to help increase sales might include:

1. The department will send out e-mails and written material to new and current customers describing the department's "enhanced" and "updated" services.
2. Each sales rep will research and find five to seven potential new customers over the next month.
3. We will offer a discount to former customers to tempt them back into using our products and services.

A word of caution, however. It's best to keep lists of goals short, containing no more than five items. Setting too many goals will only dilute their effectiveness and create confusion. Find the three or four most important goals and work on them first. Once you've achieved these goals, you can add to the list.

CONCENTRATE ON RESULTS RATHER THAN ON ACTIVITIES

Often, lists of goals focus on a series of activities rather than on the results to be achieved. For instance: "Investigate the production shortfall," "Ensure that staff are adequately trained and developed," "Prepare a recommendation on departmental staffing." These are *activities* rather than goals.

Then there's the problem of corporate-speak. "Optimize productivity ratios for the benefit of the organization," "Maximize staff morale." Sounds impressive, but what the heck does it mean? People often use words like "optimize" and "maximize" because they have no idea what can realistically be achieved and may not have thought through what needs to be done.

Goals are much clearer when they are positively stated as results. In the example from the previous paragraph you might ask, "Why am I saying we need to investigate productivity (or whatever)?" This question indicates that you must change the focus from an activity into a result. For example, "We need to investigate productivity to find out why there is a 10 percent shortfall on product X and correct that shortfall within a week." Then ask yourself, "Have I now clearly identified the actual result I need?"

GOALS SHOULD HIT THEIR MARC

Many so-called "goals" are too general to be of real use. For example, "Improve the sales of Product X." The team members responsible for selling Product X work hard and effect a 10 percent improvement in sales. Very pleased with themselves, they troop into the boss's office expecting praise, only to be greeted with, "Only 10 percent? I expected at least 15 percent, and that should have been achieved two months ago!" What went wrong?

The manager who set the goal knew what he wanted to achieve, but the goal was too general to convey the desired result to the people who had to achieve it. They worked for one result, when he wanted another.

A small mnemonic—MARC—might help you remember the essential factors in a well-crafted goal:

Measurable. A goal should be measurable to ensure that the person knows when he has achieved it. Some things are easier to measure than others. The measurement can be subjective: "Provide an adequate personnel service to internal customers." You can measure the goal by asking those customers periodically about the service.

Achievable. The goal should be seen as achievable by the person designated to carry it out. One person's challenge can be another's impossibility if their respective levels of skill or knowledge are markedly different. In the modern workplace, results are often achieved through a collaboration with personnel not under your direct control. You should not shy away from establishing goals in these cases but rather call upon your skills of managing without authority. (There are several books on the latter topic, one of the more recent being *Results Without Authority: Controlling a Project When the Team Doesn't Report to You* by Tom Kendrick.)

Results-oriented. Ensure that objectives are stated as results, not activities (see "Concentrate on Results Rather Than on Activities" on page 34). Give a deadline by which the results must be achieved.

Clear. The goal must be understood (and agreed on) by the person responsible for achieving it.

PRIORITIZE FOR MAXIMUM EFFECT

Have you ever found yourself in a situation where you have several things to do, but you know that in the time available you cannot attend to all of them satisfactorily? That's called "a clash of priorities." Often to the harassed manager it seems like all the pressing matters are priorities. If you ask your own manager which of these tasks is more important you may get a nonanswer: "They all are." So it's up to you to decide or make a best guess.

You can avoid this problem. When discussing a list of goals, include a column headed "Priority," and rate each goal as "high," "medium," or "low." Bear in mind that "low" does not mean "unimportant"; it just means less important than the "mediums" or "highs." In the event of a clash of priorities, the "highs" automatically take precedence. Most of the time your employees won't need to refer questions of priority back to you. Upfront identification of tasks as medium and low priorities makes it easy to reprioritize what can "move off your plate" as other, more pressing tasks materialize. One final point to note is that priorities of ongoing objectives can alter over time, so review priority ratings regularly.

ENCOURAGE YOUR TEAM TO SUGGEST THEIR OWN GOALS

Some managers believe that the only person who should set goals for the team is the manager herself. So goals are handed down, rather like the two tablets of stone given to Moses on Mount Sinai, with little opportunity for discussion. There are two reasons behind this thinking:

1. "It's my responsibility as the manager."
2. "If I ask them to do it, they will set themselves easy goals that won't achieve what I need."

As a manager, you are certainly responsible for ensuring that the goal is set, but that doesn't necessarily mean *you* have to set it. As for the second point, it is a natural fear but is usually unfounded. Most people like a challenge and, if asked, will usually suggest complex but realistic objectives for themselves.

You need commitment to the goals, rather than simple acceptance. The best way of ensuring this commitment is to involve the team members in setting their objectives.

Prior to any discussion of goals, ask them to think first about the key results areas in their job and then to suggest some objectives they can set. Let them think about these things and then discuss them further. It will also help if you explain MARC (see page 35).

The discussion then becomes an exchange of views—yours and the employees'. Wherever possible, agree to the employee's proposed goal if it meets your needs and is realistic for her. If her objective does not meet your requirements, you will need to explain (and prove) why, so that she learns for the next time.

The manager should also encourage and provide motivation to the staff regarding their ability to achieve "stretch goals," objectives that are seemingly unattainable using current resources. Develop an environment where risk-taking—and giving team members the knowledge, tools, and support to think creatively—is fundamental to achieving stretch goals.

PLAN ONLY THE 20 PERCENT

Have you ever worked with someone who appears to spend most of his time planning what to do rather than actually doing it? He seems to have plans for everything, even replacement dates for the pencils in the stationery cupboard! Interestingly, far more detail seems to go into the little plans than the big ones.

We all accept that planning is important, but if you try to plan everything, you will probably end up with mountains of paper that are of little real use to your job as a manager. You'll also find you have little time to do anything else. The solution is to apply the 80:20 rule. Plan the important 20 percent, that is, the 20 percent that most directly relates to the tasks at hand.

Comprehensive plans should exist for all goals pertaining to key results areas. The plan should show the main tasks necessary to achieve goals that must be successfully completed to move the plan ahead. Taking the example of moving: "Arranging for a moving company" would be a primary task, while "arranging for the electric meter to be read" would not. More planning effort should therefore go into booking the moving company because if they fail to turn up, you can't move. Failure to have the electric meter read does not stop you from moving. Also recognize the interdependencies between tasks. For instance task A (moving) must be completed before task B (installing Internet connections) can start. Task A then becomes critical because if it is not accomplished, the project will either be derailed or other aspects of the project will have to be accomplished in less time to maintain the schedule.

One method of planning projects is to divide tasks into "big" and "medium" rocks. Those assigned those tasks then have the task of defining the lower-level tasks ("pebbles" and then "sand").

MAKE SOMEONE RESPONSIBLE FOR EACH TASK, AND SET A DEADLINE

Consider the plans you already have. In addition to essential tasks:

- Do they also show who is responsible for the various tasks?
- Do they show the deadline for each task?

Many plans leave out these important elements. In worst-case scenarios the people who have to carry out the plan aren't even given a copy! Without specific responsibilities, confusion can easily arise . . . "I thought you were doing that part!" Without specific deadlines for each main task, the whole plan can easily slip behind and then fail to achieve the original goal. For each specific task:

- Decide and agree on a single person who will be responsible for ensuring that this particular task is successfully achieved. Joint responsibilities are risky, for they can lead to confusion.
- Decide and agree on the deadline by which that task must be successfully completed. As the individual selected will have responsibility for ensuring that the task is completed and done so on time, their commitment is usually vital. So agree on the goals with them at the planning stage.

SPOT THE BOMBS

Most people are capable of planning. The difficulty centers on making the plan work, that is, successfully completing all of the plan's components so that the overall goal is achieved.

It's sort of like the saying, "You make plans and God (or whatever higher power) laughs." The plan *says* what should happen, but ask yourself how many of your plans go right from start to finish? But as we all know "life happens," and sometimes it throws a bomb into even our most brilliant plans.

But, you might wonder, who can anticipate everything? Still some people seem to be unable to anticipate anything, even obvious time bombs (like expecting the movers to appear exactly within the designated appointment "window" when the person has scheduled an appointment at the new place to have the phone and cable lines installed an hour later). They have blind faith in their ability to handle anything that arises and as a result, many of their plans do not work.

A more realistic approach would be to allow for a margin of error. That is, movers usually take much longer than anticipated, so anything that needs to be done at the new place should probably be scheduled the day before or after the move. Accept reality (the existence of "life happening") and that it is better to anticipate and deal with the most serious bombs rather than simply to wait for them to explode.

By recognizing problem areas at the planning stage, you may be able to decide what can be done to handle them before they actually occur. Identifying potential problem areas or time bombs is vital to insuring that the plan will in fact take effect.

PREVENT, RATHER THAN FIGHT FIRES

In the last section, we referred to the need to search for the potential bombs that can ruin even the best plans. Some people seem to be terrific firefighters. They come into their own during a crisis and are seen by some as Mr. or Ms. Fixit. There is a lot of good publicity in firefighting if it is done successfully. Fixit rushes in with the fire extinguisher and the building is saved with minimum damage. Hooray for Fixit!

So the Fixits of the world thrive, and the fire is out. But the question still remains, should that fire have been allowed to start in the first place? Frequently the answer is that it should not. All that was needed was some initial thought about potential causes.

It is impossible, though, to anticipate everything, and equally impossible to prevent everything. For example, how do you stop a key member of the team from becoming sick at a critical stage of the project? You probably can't.

However, there are some things you *can* do to define the chief sources of potential problems:

- Decide on which actions are realistically preventable. For example, you might prevent board rejection of a proposal by finding out beforehand what the directors' criteria are.
- Decide what "firefighting" actions should be taken for problems you cannot prevent. For example, to lessen the impact of a project leader being absent (for whatever reason) at a critical stage, ensure that she designates an assistant, who will take over in the leader's absence, from the start.

CONTROL THE KEY 20 PERCENT OF TASKS IN A PLAN

As mentioned earlier, planning the 20 percent is most important. It is equally important to control that 20 percent during the plan's execution. Controlling everything is an impossible task, yet some people try! There are also managers who are continually checking on everything. Interestingly, they seem to concentrate more on the really minor issues—changing one innocuous word in a report, for example, rather than moving on to the important things. It may be easier for them to focus on minutia rather than dealing with the larger problem.

You can, however, control the key 20 percent that will produce 80 percent of the results you need. To aid control, ensure that, if possible, the information is permanently visible rather than buried in a dusty old filing cabinet (or even in the depths of a dusty high-tech computer).

One sales director had a very simple graph on his office wall. One line showed "Sales revenue," the other line, "Cost of sales." Next to the graph he placed the most recent letter from a customer—complimentary or otherwise. In his view, these factors represented the key 20 percent. The first item on the agenda of his regular sales management meetings was to always review these factors and decide on appropriate actions.

TAKE-AWAY POINTS

This chapter focused on two important aspects of goal setting: How to determine results, and how to achieve them.

For determining results:
- Initially decide upon the key results.
- Focus on results rather than on activities.
- Follow the MARC principle when setting goals.
- Prioritize to ensure that effort goes into the important matters.
- Encourage your team to suggest their own goals.

For achieving results:
- Don't try to plan everything—only the key 20 percent.
- Make someone responsible for each task, and set a deadline.
- Spot the potential problem areas beforehand.
- Prevent fires rather than fight them.
- Control the key 20 percent of tasks in a plan.

In setting goals, remember to break them down into small, manageable pieces. You will begin to discern a pattern and identify specific areas needing attention. You can then decide on which actions will help you achieve your goal and/or solve the problem.

CHAPTER 4

Making Your Day More Productive

To describe basic principles of time management

To help managers understand the importance of prioritizing

To help you organize your day

To offer alternatives in planning for the unexpected

INTRODUCTION

Some people rush from one crisis to another. They are late for appointments and meetings, forget to do things, and are never available. Others seem to have a life, and their lives, both at work and at home, seem well organized. They accomplish a lot, yet are still able to find the time to sit and talk! How do they manage their time so well? An old adage states: "If you want something done, give it to the busy person." We would change "busy" to "effective," as the two terms do not necessarily mean the same thing.

In this context, time management can be defined as "making the most productive use out of the time you spend at work." Some of the ideas can apply equally well to home life.

Are there ever enough hours in the day to do everything you want? Unfortunately, no one's yet discovered the thirty-five-hour day. Each day has only twenty-four hours, and the challenge is to make the best use of them. You have to ensure that what should be done *is* done, and that you are still able to cope with the unexpected extras that come along and that often seem to be designed to wreck your plans.

This chapter will help you to organize your time more effectively and still be able to deal with the unexpected.

SET A GOOD EXAMPLE

Most people have at least some difficulty in managing their time. When difficulties arise, we sometimes start apportioning blame:

- "They moved the goal posts on me again!"
- "He always wants everything yesterday."
- "If only I wasn't interrupted every five minutes, I could actually do some work."
- "I've spent the whole day answering the phone."

We all do it, but have you noticed how simple it is to blame everyone or everything else for difficulty in handling your time?

"So are you saying that it is all my own fault, then?" you might ask. Of course not! Our job and the people we work with make demands on our time, but "blame" isn't the issue here. Assigning blame might make us feel better, but doesn't solve the problem.

The solution to effective time management lies in your *attitude*. People who admit they have difficulty with time management will be 90 percent closer to solving the problem when they take responsibility for their own actions. There are only so many hours in a day, and it's up to you how to spend them—either doing the work that's supposed to be done or letting interruptions and other distractions take time away from what you need to do. No improvement is likely, however, unless you recognize that the only person who can positively change anything on this score is *you*.

It is very difficult to change the habits and practices of others. So ask yourself what you do (or don't do) that contributes to the problem. And how you, personally, can change the situation. Write down some possible solutions. You'll likely find you have more control than you initially thought, and you can at least do something to help remedy the problem.

URGENT IS NOT NECESSARILY IMPORTANT

It's amazing how easily we confuse "urgent" with "important." For example, what happens when the phone rings? Ninety-nine percent of the time, you pick it up. Telephones seem to have a way of instilling a feeling of urgency; by the very act of their ringing, they demand to be answered. But the telephone itself isn't the problem. Rather, it's the issue being conveyed by the caller, often some "urgent" but minor problem. Just because something is "urgent" doesn't mean it's always important. Yet because of their very immediacy, and the fact that they often center on deadlines, urgent items always seem to gain priority.

So how do we separate the wheat from the chaff so to speak, the urgent from the important? First, try not simply to react to pressure over an urgent item. Add it to your "To do" list and prioritize it (high, medium, or low), based on both "urgency" and "importance." Deal with other items in the same way, remembering that:

- High urgency is the need for something to be done immediately.
- High importance is that which relates to a crucial objective— that is, something with a real impact.

Then look at your "To do" list and decide in what order the various tasks should be done. Tasks high in both urgency and importance are done immediately, with the necessary time spent on them. Items that are urgent but unimportant should be done quickly but without the need to spend much time on them. It might help to set a time limit for each item.

Also note tasks that are important but not urgent—training and maintenance activities, for instance. Make sure to schedule these tasks so they are not "moved to the side" by urgent and/or unimportant tasks.

WRITE IT DOWN—AND MAKE IT REAL

"To do" lists would be a wonderful invention if only they didn't seem to grow faster than we can reduce them. Some people believe "To do" lists ought to be written on a roll of toilet paper because they just get longer and longer. Not only a practical thought but a recyclable one!

Most people keep some sort of list of things to do—in a book, on "Post-it" notes, and so forth. Not only can these become cumbersome, they can also be lost. "I had a little note about that here somewhere" . . . searching frantically through mounds of paper. There are a couple of ways to handle a "To do" list. The first would be to put down tasks in a diary, either electronic or paper. The list would then be in the same place as your appointments and meetings.

This approach has two advantages:

1. The list is less likely to be mislaid—unless you lose your diary!
2. By assigning the tasks to particular days, they are more visible—most people usually look at a diary at least daily. Therefore, you're more likely to accomplish the tasks when they should be done rather than leaving them to the last minute.

"But what if I don't do, or finish, something?" you might ask. Write it into the next available day. Duplication irritates, so there is a built-in motivation to get it done, rather than keep rewriting some task or other. A second way to handle a "to do" list that I've had success with is to purchase a wipe-off bulletin board and place it prominently in my workspace. I see it daily and can keep track of various projects. There is also a sense of satisfaction when I wipe out a task (though of course it will be replaced with a new one).

Regardless of which system you use, the act of ticking or crossing off each task provides a feeling of accomplishment and also reminds you what there is left to do that day. An added benefit of recording all of the tasks is that it reduces any worry that you will forget to do something. Although you may never complete all of the tasks, it will not be because you forgot but because you chose to complete another activity.

Any System Is Fine As Long As It Is Yours

Let's face it: There's a lot of pressure to purchase the latest "bell and whistle" that will supposedly help us master time, whether it's an electronic system, an all-in-one cell phone, or an expensive leather planner. Shell out a few hundred dollars, and *voila*—your time-management problems will be solved!

If only . . . All too often these systems force you into doing things the manufacturer's way, which may not achieve what you want or may be so complicated that you are wasting time figuring out how to plan your day. Consequently, only a small part of the system is actually used if it's used at all.

In truth, any system will work, as long as it's compatible with your work habits. For example, I use a Palm Pilot that's several years old and have (so far) resisted the seemingly inevitable Black-Berry, Treo, and/or iPhone. If writing a "To do" list on the back of an envelope works, then do that. Likewise, if using a very expensive leather-bound system makes you feel good and spurs you to manage your time more effectively, that's fine too. Bottom line: it must suit you and your work habits and style. But if your present system leaves something to be desired, first, jot down what any new system must do for you. Then, and only then, look at the available options, including that of modifying your existing system.

If you do use a computerized time-management system make sure it can "sync" or "beam" with your calendar. That way all records will be consistent and you'll avoid writing everything down twice (which in itself can lead to errors).

DON'T RUSH AROUND AIMLESSLY—ORGANIZE A ROUTINE DAY

Have you noticed how some people appear to be more organized than others? They react immediately to every call on their time—the latest demand is always the one they tackle right now.

However, what we should be doing is often different from what we actually are accomplishing!

Certainly there are those who enjoy jumping on every situation, "firing from the hip." But while that might give the odd adrenaline rush, it is not necessarily effective. Most of us enjoy some sensible pressure and often feel that we perform best under these circumstances. What happens, though, if that pressure becomes permanent? It either becomes normal so it ceases to have the motivational effect, or it puts us into stress overload, resulting in burnout. Neither is effective.

There are, in most jobs, a series of routine tasks that must be done regularly—read the mail, check and sign the expenses, prepare the monthly report, and so on. These tasks are usually fairly boring. Some of us look for any excuse to do something far more interesting and enjoyable, and reacting to demands can seem a justifiable way of avoiding mundane tasks . . . "Sorry, I didn't finish the report as I spent most of the day helping Jane with that computer problem." The truth is, we enjoyed dealing with the problem more than writing the report, so the routine matter suffered.

However, you can get to everything that needs to be done by spending the first ten minutes of your working day dividing tasks into two areas: deciding what you *must* do and which you would *like to* do, if there is time. If appropriate, plan to do the routine (boring) items first. Having completed those, reward yourself with something interesting or enjoyable.

DEALING WITH OFFICE POLITICS AND INTERRUPTIONS

It's the 80:20 rule yet again . . . 80 percent of our interruptions are caused by 20 percent of the people.

Have you ever been sitting at your desk and seen a team member heading in your direction and thought, "Oh no. Not them, not today, *Please!*" They arrive, grab the nearest chair, make themselves comfy, and you know you are in for a long session!

The difficulty is that until they start to talk, you have no idea how important their subject is. If it is urgent or important, the interruption is valid. However, what do you do if they want to discuss their vacation or their grandkid, but you are desperately trying to prepare a presentation due in ten minutes? Once they are seated and comfortable, they are very hard to get rid of!

The answer is simple: As they approach your desk, stand up. For most people, your body language will convey that sitting in the visitor's chair is inappropriate at this time. At most the person might perch on the corner of your desk, but that's not a particularly comfortable spot and gives them an incentive to leave. You can then say something along the lines of "Morning, David. What can I do for you?" David's reply should tell you what you need to know. You can then invite him to sit down or suggest talking later.

Office politics and organizational matters can also wreak havoc with time management. Workday parties celebrating birthdays, promotions, and other events, even company-wide meetings that deal with general policy matters can all throw a wrench into your well-planned day. If possible, stay for a few minutes, then excuse yourself, unless the meeting is essential to the performance of your job or your role as a manager. If the meeting's about organizational restructuring, for instance, employees will have questions, and you'll need to be available to answer them.

Even though most of us play office politics in one form or another, remember you have control of your level of involvement there as well. You can stand around the water cooler and chat, or you can bring your own bottled water and get your work done.

Still another time issue facing managers is what's known as "monkey jumping." This occurs when an employee or associate plops himself down, relates a problem (a monkey on his back, so to speak), and expects it to become yours—that is, he transfers the monkey from his arena to yours! Savvy managers should take care of the "monkey" right on the spot, suggesting ways for the problem to be solved and if appropriate, requesting feedback on any actions taken as a result of their suggestion(s).

EXPECT THE UNEXPECTED

Consider a recent daily plan and ask yourself whether you completed it. If you only did most or some of it, why was that? The most likely reason your plan was wrecked was because of unexpected demands on your time. "Hold on though," you may say. "With the best will in the world, I can't plan for the unexpected, can I?" In fact, you can.

Ask yourself how much work you actually planned to do in eight hours. Many daily plans appear to allocate something close to eight hours' work to be done in an eight-hour day. In other words, there's no leeway for the unexpected, and when it does arise, the plan is disrupted. How realistic is it to plan eight full hours of work during an eight-hour day?

One to two hours—maybe more—of your day are likely to be spent "putting out fires." You can't plan for the actual tasks that arise, but you can allocate time for the unexpected! Keep a log for a few days to see how much time you spend on unforeseen tasks.

Once you get an average figure, allow for it in your daily plans. Suppose that handling unanticipated issues takes two hours each day. Plan for about six hours' worth of work. Although such planning is an inexact science, you are more likely to accomplish the designated tasks because you've set them within a more realistic time frame.

AVOID PLAYING DESK CHESS

You are going through your in-basket and come to a tricky item. "Mmmm," you think. "Not sure what to do with this one." You place it on the top left part of your desk. Later in the day it is still there, and you feel guilty. You are still unsure what to do with it so you move it to the bottom right . . . "That's better. At least I have done something." Eventually after several unproductive moves around the desk, you put it into some secret place (bottom drawer?)

reserved for such items and hope nobody asks for it. This is playing "desk chess." Several ideas might help you "win" at desk chess:

- Pick out the items you play "desk chess" with. Every time you move one of these items around the desk, punch a hole in the top corner. This will reveal the culprits!
- Ask yourself what will happen if you don't act on that particular matter. Any decision could be better than none.
- Figure out if more information is needed. Make that phone call to request the information, and put the file in your "Awaiting Reply" tray.
- If the task is just difficult or uninteresting, just do it, but reward yourself afterward by taking a coffee break or do something else that's pleasurable.

Some managers play a similar version of this game with e-mail, of which most managers receive overwhelming amounts. Ideally you should take care of it on the spot, filing, responding to, or tagging e-mail as it comes in. However, if you let it pile up, one way to deal with it is to sort it by subject and delete all but the most recent e-mail on that particular subject. (There's a chance you might miss an important comment, but given the fact that most e-mails are "copied" from earlier e-mails, the probability is relatively small.)

LEARN HOW TO SAY "NO" CONSTRUCTIVELY

In every office, there are the well-meaning folk who can't say "no." They take on too much and easily go into overload. In short, they are put upon! They try very hard to do everything but end up spending most of their time doing things for everyone else and not enough on their own work. Certainly other people view them as helpful and like them, but just consider how this habit affects their productivity. Is helping everyone else a valid excuse not to get the job done?

At the opposite end of the spectrum are those who always say "no" and are ruthless about it. They probably complete their own work but are seen by others as decidedly unhelpful and are often avoided and disliked.

As a manager, do you fit into either category? Everyone recognizes that we all occasionally have to say "no" if we are to complete our own work satisfactorily and in time. However, consider the following approach:

1. Don't say "no" all of the time.
2. When you do have to say "no," say it constructively.

For example, when a team member has a serious problem on some very important task, try to reorganize your schedule to help. Check, though, that the situation is critical and not simply panic on their part.

If you have shown that you are prepared to help when there is a genuine crisis, it is easier to say "No" when what you are doing takes priority. Always explain the reasons why you cannot respond when asked for help—that is, the importance or urgency of your own immediate task.

AVOID EXCESSIVE PAPERWORK

Do you spend much time reading or writing reams? Often, we are looking for only one or two key points. The problem is that, in order to find them, we have to read through umpteen pages or at least scan the whole document. A similar situation can apply in reverse. When we are writing a report, we often include much detail and/or justification on the grounds that "they might need this information."

The first question must of course be: "Do I need to read or write this anyway?" If not, don't! Too much paper goes to people who don't need (or want) it.

However, let's assume that you do need to read or write regular reports. In this case, consider applying the Churchill Principle, which is (slightly modified): "Tell me, on one side of one sheet of paper only, what I need to know." If you are the recipient of regular reports, consider whether a one-sheet summary of key points will do the trick. If so, tell the author. It will save her time in writing as well. Similarly, if you are going to write a regular report, find out whether a one-sheet summary of key points will be sufficient for the receiver. On those occasions when more detail is needed as backup, you can often provide this over the phone.

TAKE-AWAY POINTS

- Ultimately, you are responsible for your own time. Remember, the busiest people are often the best time managers.
- Effective time managers lead by example. Accepting responsibility for your time issues is the first step to achieving control of your time.
- Don't confuse "urgent" with "important." Make sure you understand the difference, and prioritize these tasks.
- Write everything you need to do in a place you see every day. Use a planning system that works for you, even if it's as low tech as jotting a list on paper and sticking it on a bulletin board.
- Every day has its own "brush fires." Understand that sometimes putting them out is just a way of avoiding boring tasks. Make sure to stick to and organize a basic routine.
- Plan for the unexpected by keeping a record of interruptions so you can gauge how much time they'll take in an average day and arrange your workload around that.
- Employ tactful ways of dealing with office politics and interruptions that can steal valuable time from your workday.
- Avoid "desk chess"—moving around things you'd rather not deal with—and instead tackle such issues directly. Reward yourself after you've got the job done.

- Learn how to say "no" constructively and "yes" when it's really needed.
- Use the Churchill Principle whenever possible by keeping reports and paperwork to one page that summarizes key points.

CHAPTER 5

Effective Problem-Solving

CHAPTER OBJECTIVES

To approach problem-solving and cause analysis in a constructive manner

To explain the basic principles and importance of problem-solving and cause analysis

To help you to find the real cause of a problem

INTRODUCTION

The term *problem solving* can itself cause problems. People use it to combine two distinct things: finding out why a problem exists, then fixing it. However, these two processes can also be separate: that is, finding out what the cause is (cause analysis, discussed in this chapter) is different from deciding on the best course of action (Chapter 6).

A deviation from normal can be positive or negative. For example, it is probably just as important to find out why a member of the team is performing so well as it is to find out why, say, the reject rate for a product has gone up.

However, decision-making does not always follow cause analysis. As well, you may need to make a decision without any problem to solve, for instance in choosing who to promote to manage a new section. Alternatively, you may want to find out why something is happening in a situation where someone else will subsequently have to make the decision about what to do—investigating a situation on behalf of another manager because you have technical expertise is one example.

FOR EVERY ACTION, THERE IS A REACTION

Roget's New Millennium Thesaurus[10] defines a problem as, "botheration, box, complication, crunch, dilemma, disagreement, dispute, disputed point, doubt, headache, hitch, holy mess, hot potato, hot water, issue, mess, nut, obstacle, pickle, predicament, quandary, question, scrape, squeeze, trouble . . ." and so on. But the most common term for "problem" in current corporate-speak is "issue," which sort of bubble-wraps itself around the situation to make it seem less harsh.

For example, if someone says, "I have some issues with that," he'll likely get a less negative or defensive reaction than if he bluntly states, "I have a problem with that." Right off the bat, the word *problem* can send out red flags.

Nowhere is this truer than in dealing with customer service people. Call them up on the phone, guns blazing and angry about a particular situation, and they'll be a lot less willing to help and offer a satisfactory solution. However if you approach them tactfully, in team mode ("This situation is a real mess and I'd like to see if you can help me"), they'll be more willing to provide a solution. The same is true of your employees. The trick is to maintain a sense of perspective and "cool," especially before you have all the facts (usually easier in the workplace than in dealing with customer service representatives).

In handling a problem or issue, take the tack that you need to know why something is happening in order to reinforce it (if it is positive) or correct it (if it is negative). You don't want to take action without knowing the cause, or you may get a reaction that isn't at all in conjunction with what's actually going on. Assume nothing until you have all the facts.

CLEARLY SEPARATE CAUSE FROM EFFECT

Cause analysis has, by definition, to deal with cause and effect. Sometimes people do not separate cause and effect or become so confused that they attempt to deal with the effect rather than the cause.

The problem is that a cause can itself be an effect of an even deeper cause. Where, then, do you stop? The following might help to illustrate the difficulty:

- The oil burner at home breaks down, which was caused by . . .
- The oil pump malfunctioning, which was caused by . . .
- Faulty wiring, which was caused by . . .
- The electrician not putting in correct wiring, which was caused by . . .
- Poor training of the electrician, and so on.

As you can see, replacing the pump is dealing with the effect, and it would solve the problem only temporarily until the wiring went again. Our action in this case is too superficial. Yet at the other (lower) end of the problem, you probably can't do much about your electrician's training! The most practical solution, therefore, is to ask an electrician to re-wire the system.

So the next logical question is: "How far do I need to go back to solve this problem for all practical purposes?" This is where you'll need clarity as to where your responsibility ends and others' begins. Identify those causes of problems upon which you can take, or initiate, some form of action.

BUILD UPON A SOLID STARTING POINT

When looking at a deviation from normal, having a good set of starting blocks—that is, a sound basis to begin from—is essential. All too often we generalize far too easily and even give titles to some of the bigger or longer-term problems: the invoicing issue, the sales dispute, the absentee problem, and so on. Everyone believes they know what is meant by each term, but often individuals have very different views that don't always match. Take the invoicing issue, for example. One administrator might see it as a need for more motivated staff to process the invoices more quickly, while the invoicing manager might view it as a requirement for better computer facilities. The sales manager regards it as the reason why the invoices are often incorrect, while the invoicing clerk looks upon it as management expecting the impossible.

Setting the starting blocks correctly helps an athlete avoid false or bad starts. The same applies with cause analysis: if the right start is made, the rest becomes easier and you don't have to make up for lost time. Before beginning any detailed analysis find out exactly what deviation you are trying to analyze and ask:

- What or who is involved?
- Exactly what is the deviation from normal?

By applying these questions to the "invoicing issue," you can track the processes invoices go through and which ones are late, thus beginning to define the cause of the problem.

Deviations can also be positive, so you can apply the same principles to define the starting blocks for those as well.

DEFINE THE PROBLEM EFFECTIVELY, AND BE SPECIFIC

"Effectively" means being systematic about collecting relevant information. Often the first step is to jot down everything we know about the issue—data, probable causes, more data, possible actions, and so forth, all mixed up together.

Cause analysis must be systematic, otherwise there is the danger of going down blind alleys only to find—sometimes much later—that we have to return to the main route. Moreover, there is little point in trying to check a possible cause until we have some facts against which to judge whether it is the real reason or not.

First, decide if you already know why the issue exists. If you are absolutely sure you know the cause, then you don't need cause analysis. If you don't know or are unsure, use the following to guide you in systematically collecting data about the issue.

- What is happening?
- When does it happen?
- How does it show up?

- Where is it happening?
- Who is involved?

When collecting data about the deviation (good or bad), people again tend to generalize. Suppose, for example, there is a problem with invoices going out late. Questions from the previous paragraph might generate the following answers:

- What?—invoices
- Why?—not too sure, might be the computer
- When?—this quarter
- How?—at management meeting
- Where?—Accounts department
- Who?—Accounts staff

This information is too general to be of much practical use, so delve deeper by asking specific, pointed questions. If you are trying to get information from others who are generalizing, try adding the word *exactly* with each question.

- What (exactly)?—all invoices for furniture over $1,500 going out ten days late
- Why (exactly)?—the cause is unknown
- When (exactly)?—since March 1 of this year
- How (exactly)?—reported by invoicing section leader at meeting on March 30
- Where (exactly)?—invoicing section, Accounts department
- Who (exactly)?—only those staff in the section who deal with furniture invoices over $1,500

USE CHARTS AND DIAGRAMS TO HELP

When trying to define a problem, words alone can be restrictive. Sometimes it is difficult to discern what is happening, or where.

We have all heard the phrase "One picture is worth a thousand words." In the case of cause analysis, a picture or diagram can also save a thousand words!

A *chart* or *diagram* can further help to define the problem by providing additional information. Not only will it help clearly delineate who has done what, but it also can sort information into relevant clusters of data. For instance, a bar graph can show the varying rates of product return from month to month, allowing you to determine if there is a trend that must be addressed.

Other types of useful charts are:

- Line graph—depicts the connection between two sets of data, one represented vertically and the other, horizontally. The relationship is defined where the two scales intersect.
- Bar chart—similar to a graph, but with shaded blocks instead of a plotting line.
- Pie chart—shows data in proportion to one another.
- Frequency list—counts the number of times an activity occurs so that the daily/weekly/monthly frequency can be identified.

Pictorial depictions can also help spot trends as well as provide a different point of view, giving us insights that we might otherwise miss.

AVOID ASSUMPTIONS WHEN DEALING WITH PEOPLE

In his book, *The Four Agreements*,[11] Don Miguel Ruiz advises against making assumptions in any situation. He provides an example of encountering someone you have a crush on at the mall. The person smiles at you and walks away, giving you a sense that she likes you back, creating an entire relationship that in fact may only exist in your mind.

This example applies to the workplace as well. By assuming that X person always reacts in a certain way or is at the bottom of a particular problem, you are merely assigning blame, rather than dealing with the facts.

Ruiz recommends dealing with assumptions by asking questions. "Have the courage to ask questions until you are clear as you can be, and even then do not assume you know all there is to know about a given situation," he writes. Of course, you can't check everything. But if you make assumptions, make sure they are credible; that is, they have at least some basis in hard facts.

Cause analysis relies on facts, so identify any assumptions in the data and check to see whether they are correct. On occasions where you cannot verify a given point, mark the data in some way to show that it is an assumption rather than fact.

DEVIATIONS ARE CAUSED BY CHANGES

Having collected the data, we now need to try and identify possible causes of the problem. For any deviation there could be many possibilities. For starters, you might want to look at the changes that have occurred in the categories of human resources, machinery or systems, and methods or procedures. Then examine inputs to the process such as raw materials and how the work comes to a group.

What sometimes happens is that people hold a personal or group brainstorming-type session to generate various possibilities, asking: "What could possibly cause this situation?"

The resulting list can be enormous, and it will take a long time to check each one. What is needed is some concept or method that reduces the list of possibilities to those likely to have a direct bearing on the problem.

This is where Newton's first law of motion comes in. The law states: "Every body continues in a state of rest or uniform motion in a straight line unless acted upon by an external impressed force." This concept—that most things go along uninterrupted until some outside force comes along and disturbs it—is the real key to effective cause analysis. Say, for example, my cat Savannah is sleeping (at rest) on my desk. I reach over and pet her (an external force), causing her to wake up and move.

Try to identify what relevant changes have occurred at or around the time the deviation first arose. It will also help to note when the change occurred. Then you can generate possible causes from these changes. For example, suppose there was a change in the computer system. The possible cause might be: "The new computer system is faulty, making incorrect calculations."

FINDING THE REAL OR UNDERLYING CAUSE

Now you have a list of possible causes. It is fairly unlikely that they all caused the deviation, but how do you decide which causes are at the bottom of the issue?

A problem-solving group can divide into subgroups, each of which takes a possible cause to check on and report back. This represents a logical division of labor, but is it really necessary to spend so much time modifying everything to see the effect?

Other groups might pick the particular cause they like the look of and go off to remedy that. Fine, if they have chosen the right cause, but how much time and money is wasted if it's not?

What is needed is some method of "eliminating the impossible," as Sherlock Holmes would say.

> *How often have I said to you that when you have eliminated the impossible, whatever remains, however improbable, must be the truth?*
>
> Sir Arthur Conan Doyle, *The Sign of the Four*

Take each of the possible causes and compare each one with the "what, why, when, how, where, and who" data you collected. Ask whether that cause would explain all of the facts you have. For example, if one possible cause is "a glitch in the new computer system," if the system was changed *after* the problem first arose, that eliminates that cause!

When you have eliminated the impossible via this approach, whatever is left must be the truth, or at least pretty close to it.

What if you eliminate everything? Either one or more of your facts are wrong, or you have missed a change somewhere along the line.

WHEN THERE MAY BE MORE THAN ONE CAUSE

Consider the following problem: *Production of car components has fallen by 20 percent.* After cause analysis, the production manager is left with several possible causes that cannot be entirely eliminated:

- Faulty batch of raw material (metal rods) delivered.
- Quality standards (tolerances on dimensions) now more stringent, causing more scrap.
- Reduced productivity due to unfounded rumors of an unfriendly takeover.
- Increased checking by Quality Control, increasing reject rate.

It might help to prioritize action by asking the following:

- Which is the *root cause*—the one that directly produces the problem?
- Which are *contributory causes*—those that contribute to the problem but do not directly cause it?

In the example, the root cause is more stringent quality standards, which are found to be unrealistic for the relatively old machines in the factory. Consequently, production of "good" components fell by 20 percent. The other factors contributed to the problem but did not actually cause it. The rumors of a takeover were a direct result of uncertainty engendered by the reduced production output, while the faulty material only applied to one day's production. The higher reject rates meant more frequent checking by the inspectors.

When investigating multiple causes, remember to follow the thread of events and keep asking questions until you find the single, major contributing factor. In this case, all roads lead back to the outdated machinery, and the fact that it could not produce components that met updated standards.

TAKE-AWAY POINTS

- Problems are caused by deviations, which in themselves can be positive or negative. Effective managers do cause analysis on both kinds to improve processes and productivity.
- In tackling problems or issues, phrase them in the positive and take a team approach. Make sure you have all the facts before coming to conclusions.
- Separate cause from effect and dig out underlying causes until you find those that you have control over and can find solutions for.
- Determine your starting point then systematically start asking specific questions pertaining to who, what, where, when, why, and how.
- Charts, diagrams, and other pictorial data can help you sort and organize information efficiently, provide new insights, and help spot trends.
- Try to avoid assumptions. If you must make assumptions, make sure they are credible.
- Deviations can have one cause or many. First, try to identify what relevant changes occurred at or around the time the deviation first arose. Then use the process of elimination to locate the root, or basic, cause.

CHAPTER 6

How to Make Decisions

To explain the difference between "logical" and "creative" decision-making

To teach managers how to determine risks and benefits and set criteria

To help managers with decision-making, both long term and immediate

To provide guidance as to effective brainstorming sessions

INTRODUCTION

Decision-making can be a tricky management skill. Many people seem to think that they only make a few choices; they associate decision-making solely with important matters. But the truth is, probably less than 20 percent of our decisions fall into the "important" category. We make many other decisions—the remaining 80 percent—on more "routine" matters. (It's that 80:20 rule again!) Although routine decisions are made quickly, some thought does go into them. They're just done more or less on automatic pilot, using simpler thought processes. Managers are called upon to make many decisions. This chapter will provide ideas as to how to handle them.

LOGICAL VERSUS CREATIVE DECISION-MAKING

Logical decisions are those with a finite number of options. Your objective is to select the options that best meet the requirement. For example, choosing a new computer system falls into this category as would deciding who to promote or recruit.

The wrong choice would cause problems, and the more important the decision, the greater the problems. Imagine the costs (direct and indirect) of recruiting the wrong person.

Creative decisions are those that, as yet, have no options, so you must create them. Having generated possible options, you can then evaluate the problem or issue in much the same way as logical decisions. Decisions that fall into this category might include how to market services more widely or how to increase revenue.

Creative decisions encourage novel approaches and ideas and are vital in finding new and innovative ways to move forward.

SET CRITERIA BEFORE THINKING ABOUT THE OPTIONS

Think about a recent decision and how you went about making it. Usually you start by weighing options then comparing them to decide which one best suited your purposes. Although this method can be effective, unbeknownst to you your decision may have been *biased*.

Have you ever convinced yourself that something is the best option solely because you liked that particular choice? In fact, you may well have made up your mind unconsciously after seeing the one you like. The rest were effectively a lost cause. In cases like this, it's easy to "bend" the requirements to suit our bias—without even realizing it. For example, a friend went out to buy a minivan and came back with a two-seat sports car. His partner suggested he might need to buy a roof rack to make room for his three kids. After a couple of weeks he changed the car, but it cost him (in more ways than one)!

Everyone has biases; it's part of being human. You can, however, avoid biases resulting in bad choices by setting criteria before even considering any options. Criteria should describe the ideal you are trying to achieve. It helps to categorize these criteria as either "essential" or "desirable." For instance, if you are leasing office space, some of the criteria might be: appeal to customers and cost per square foot (essential), proximity to public transportation and length of the lease (desirable). It is perfectly fine to include likes and dislikes in your criteria, provided they are appropriate (and legal).

CONSIDER A RANGE OF OPTIONS, INCLUDING DO NOTHING

Another aspect of potential bias is to unreasonably limit the options to the one or two that you like or have worked before.

Except for "yes/no" decisions, there are rarely only just a couple of options. A manifestation of this problem is when you hear yourself (or someone else) saying, "But we have always done it this way." Fear of the unknown can easily generate unreasonable bias against new or different approaches to doing things.

At the other end of the scale, some decision-making discussions never consider the option of "Stay as we are." However, the way forward should represent an improvement on the current position. If you don't consider the current position, how can you measure improvement? If it isn't broken, why fix it?

Look at the options being generated and ask yourself whether they represent a reasonable range, including the option of "Stay as we are."

CONSIDER THE RISKS AND BENEFITS

Most people look at the benefits of available options when trying to make a decision. Some, however, seem to feel that considering the risks introduces a negative note to the proceedings. Consequently, the risks receive little, if any, attention. In some work environments people find that suggesting risks is unacceptable, so they keep quiet about them.

At the opposite end of the spectrum are those who only opt for "safe" decisions, that is, those that seem to carry minimum risk. While such decisions might seem secure, the question should be: "Will the low-risk option actually produce the best result?" There might be another, better option that has higher (though manageable) risks but far greater benefits.

Good decision-making considers both the benefits and the risks of each option. The perfect option has yet to be invented. Try to consider the severity and likelihood of the risk to indicate its significance.

Using the example of leasing office space mentioned on page 72, Option A might be near public transportation, be visually appealing to customers and have a low cost per square foot (all scoring high on the benefit scale), and have a short-term lease (making it low on the risk scale). Conversely, Option B may be lacking in visual appeal, have a high cost per square foot, and not be near public transportation making it low on the benefit scale. Even if it had the same short-term lease (making them equal on the risk scale), Option A is preferable.

Decision-making is a balancing act—weighing the benefits of each option against the risks. If there is an option with the highest benefits and least snags, the decision is easy. If, on the other hand, there is a high-benefit/high-risk option, ask whether it is possible to reduce or manage those risks in order to achieve the benefits.

EFFECTIVE GROUP DECISION-MAKING

Group decision-making can become highly emotional. One person wants Approach A; someone else is strongly in favor of Approach B. Tempers may flare when the two opposing viewpoints clash. It can turn into a power struggle, which benefits no one.

A way to circumvent this is to use the list discussed in the previous section. You can do this via black/white boards, PowerPoint presentations, flip charts, or any method designed to present each party's salient points. Ask each individual to give you their respective views, and summarize them for presentation to the entire group. Each will have his uninterrupted time to describe his position using any of the above-mentioned methods of presentation. That way, the pros and cons of each viewpoint will be enumerated, and a decision will be based on the facts—what makes most sense for the team and the organization. Such an approach invests the entire group in the decision. It is no longer about the person but the situation.

Healthy disagreement is fine and should be encouraged as long as all participants stick to facts and avoid finger pointing and accusations. If you feel that a more personal argument is about to erupt, then it's best to call a "time out." If an immediate decision is not called for, suggest that opposing parties gather pertinent information and present it at a later date.

DECIDING ON THE BASIS OF BENEFITS VERSUS SNAGS

If you ask most people how they make decisions, they will usually say something like: "I weigh up the benefits of the options, do the same with the disadvantages, then choose." If everyone uses the same decision-making processes, then why do we differ so much in our choices? Most of us have attended meetings where someone was vehemently opposed to the option we wanted, or supported an option that we would never choose. Most put this down to differences in "individual judgments." Each person believes that his or her reasoning is right. But the truth is, it's more about opinion.

When weighing up benefits versus snags, people seem to err toward one side or the other. Someone with a "glass half empty" (pessimistic) standpoint will see the disadvantages as more significant than the benefits, whereas the person with the "glass half full" (optimistic) view will see benefits as more significant than possible negative risks. Thus they will probably favor different options.

As a manager you'll need to find a mutually acceptable way of objectively evaluating both the benefits and the snags of the options via a scoring scale or a "high, medium, or low" rating. Remember, though, that the figures are only an expression of your collective judgment. These methods seem to work far better than an emotional argument born of frustration, especially when people who differ feel compelled to defend their reasoning and judgments.

YOU WILL NEVER HAVE ALL OF THE INFORMATION. DECIDE!

Making the decision itself is often one of the hardest steps that a manager can face. Some people are prepared to take risks that accompany decision-making, others are not. One question we all ask ourselves, however, is: "Do I have all the information I need?"

Some people want to dot every "i" and cross every "t" before they decide anything, in order to reduce the chances of being wrong. However, this is not only impossible but impractical. How often do you have all the information you would like? We can rarely be certain of every fact, and so many decisions are based on at least some assumptions.

Most people want to make the right decision, but they need to accept they won't get every little bit of data they would like. The question should then be rephrased to: "Do I have all the essential information to make a reasoned decision?" Decisions are often concerned to some extent with predicting the future, and some assumptions are therefore inevitable.

If you could guarantee that all your decisions were right, you would likely be at least a millionaire! (But, then so would everyone else, having figured out the same technique.) All you can hope to do is to be successful with the important ones. Since some errors are inevitable, no manager should expect perfection in decision-making.

When a decision is needed, failure to decide can be a far bigger problem than making a wrong decision. It's like the slogan from the 1960s, "Not to decide is to decide."

QUICK DECISIONS HAVE THEIR OWN SET OF RISKS

Probably 80 percent of our decisions fall into the category of quick decisions. Someone asks if she can have tomorrow off or if he can borrow the computer for a couple of hours. There are people who would give each detailed consideration, but most of us usually simply react immediately to these requests and use "gut feeling." In other words, it seems naturally right at the time. However, quick decisions do not have to mean "instant." There is usually some thinking time, even if only a minute or two. Often the options are simple: either say "yes" or "no." Perhaps more so than other types of workers, managers need to school themselves to consider two questions before making even small decisions.

1. What are the essential criteria?
2. What are the main risks on both options?

Suppose, for example, someone asks to borrow your computer this afternoon. Before automatically answering either way, you think:

- I can finish the vital report for the board by lunchtime (Criteria).
- "Yes" means I won't have computer access (Risk A), but since I'll be calling on customers I won't likely need it.
- "No" means I would possibly be seen as unhelpful (Risk B).

In this situation, the ramifications of Risk B—being seen as unhelpful—outweigh those of Risk A, which is that although you need the computer sometimes, such is not the case this afternoon. Conclusion: Agree to the request.

You might already unconsciously do something like this. But asking yourself those two quick questions before making even small decisions should help circumvent the consequences of inaction—the "deadline" passes, with all of the attendant problems—or a too-rapid "gut reaction" (you want to be nice, but you did need the computer after all and now you'll be behind on your work) that would cause more problems than it solves.

AVOID SETTING CRITERIA TOO EARLY

Everyone can be creative, but some seem to find it easier than others. People often seem to link creativity with personality traits: for example, "creative people are extroverts." While introverts may possibly be more reluctant to suggest zany solutions in a group, personality type may not be the reason for an apparent lack of creativity. Instead it may be due to a thinking style.

Certain people mentally screen out ideas by considering the criteria too early. For example, "I have this idea but the cost would probably be too high, so I won't suggest it." Consequently, a potentially useful solution has been lost. Why, then, is it potentially useful if it's too expensive? After all, someone might suggest a way of reducing the cost while retaining the chief benefit. This cannot be done if the idea is never suggested.

Do not set (or even discuss) any criteria before or during a brainstorming session whose purpose is to generate options. At this stage the objective is quantity, rather than quality, of ideas.

Explain to your team that the aim of the brainstorming session is to generate outside the suggestion box ideas and options, no matter how farfetched they may initially sound. The more practical criteria will be discussed later. Reward them for their creativity by encouraging their suggestions.

THE PITFALLS OF EVALUATING DURING BRAINSTORMING

However, some participants will still try to evaluate the ideas during a brainstorming session:

- "Hold on, Jane. That idea won't be acceptable to the board."
- "You won't be able to accomplish that in the workshop, Harry."
- "Oh, come on, be realistic, Dave. There's not enough time for that."

Comments like these will kill creativity very quickly, especially among those who are more reluctant to suggest new and different options or quieter people who might also lack confidence. They feel they are being quite brave to suggest something in the first place and will simply clam up in the face of such remarks. Even the most thick-skinned person will soon give up if he must deal with ongoing negativity. And the number of ideas will be significantly reduced.

Set a clear rule at the onset—no evaluation of others' ideas (yet). Explain why this is so important and stress that the ideas will be evaluated, but later. You might even nominate one of the team as a monitor who will stop the meeting immediately if the rule is breached.

Some people do not even realize that they are evaluating. With the inadvertent (and frequent) offender, making a light joke of it can sometimes help: "There you go again, Fred," with a smile.

ENCOURAGE IDEAS OUTSIDE THE SUGGESTION BOX

Creative or novel ideas are best nurtured in a friendly, positive, and enthusiastic atmosphere. People are more willing to open up and share their innermost feelings when there's a sense of relaxation and freedom. This is why corporate retreats and "character building" sessions have become so popular—you see new and different facets of the person outside the 9-to-5 setting. By taking you out of your zone of expectation, the situation encourages you to come up with new ideas or ways of operating.

Of course it's impractical (and expensive) to set every brainstorming session at a retreat. But if the atmosphere is serious and businesslike, people will have a tendency to play it safe and only propose tried and tested ideas that have been known to work in the past. So how do you create a mood conducive to thinking outside the suggestion box?

According to Ozone, a management consultancy firm, four things are essential to a good brainstorming session:[12]

- Criticism is ruled out—no matter how strange the idea.
- Freewheeling is welcomed—let imagination run as free as possible.
- Quantity is wanted—generate as many ideas as possible.

- Combination and improvement are sought—building on ideas of other members.

These can be done anywhere, even in the cafeteria or a meeting room. Encouraging humor and laughter is also effective in generating new ideas, as long as people are laughing with—and not at—each other. Effective managers will take notice of the difference, and circumvent the latter by pointing out the inappropriateness of making fun of others.

Out of maybe twenty suggestions there is often one gem that can be modified, but the other nineteen are needed to encourage it in the first place.

TAKE-AWAY POINTS

- With *logical decisions*, you have a finite number of options; with *creative decisions*, you must come up with your own options.
- It's important to set criteria and discern whether they are "essential" or "desirable."
- "Do nothing" is also an option. If it isn't broken, why fix it?
- Weighing risks and benefits is a balancing act, especially in a group where there are opposing points of view.
- Not to decide is to decide—you'll never have all the facts.
- On the other hand, think twice before making snap judgments or going with gut feelings—consider essential criteria and risks.
- Avoid setting criteria too early; encourage out-of-the-box thinking.
- Set brainstorming sessions in an informal, nurturing atmosphere to encourage participation from all staff members, even those who are normally reticent.
- Although the group can reach a consensus, even that can be subjective and dependent upon participants' opinions and worldview.

CHAPTER 7

Active Listening and Positive Persuasion

To clearly define oral communication and persuasion

To help managers deal with different types of situations—verbal aggression, for example—that require communications skills

To teach the essentials of persuasion

To explain the different skills needed in persuasion and negotiation

INTRODUCTION

Communication is the transfer of information from one person to another. We spend three-fourths of our waking hours communicating our knowledge, thoughts, and ideas to others. Experts believe that successful *verbal communication* depends 10 percent on what you say and 90 percent on how you say it. Yet, thanks in part to technology that allows for instant communication through e-mails, text messaging, and faxes, verbal communication is often downplayed and, in some instances, assigned the importance of a manual typewriter.

By the very nature of their responsibilities, managers must be skilled in verbal communication and persuasion. Not only must they use them effectively in dealing with their team and coworkers, but also when interacting with outside personnel, as a representative of their company. Managers need to be able to present themselves in an articulate and intelligent manner both in "real time" and from a distance, via phone, e-mail, and other forms of communication.

ORAL COMMUNICATION AND PERSUASION

Not only does effective *oral communication* mean speaking clearly and concisely it also means ensuring that information is passed on to and understood by the recipient. Many people speak clearly, yet communication so often fails because what is said is either incorrectly heard or not properly understood. Managers have to "get things done through others," and in order for this to happen, everyone must understand what is required—that is, they must be "on the same page" (even if it is a Web page!).

Persuasion is the ability to get other people to do what you need, willingly if possible, but certainly without resorting to coercion. The ability to persuade is vital to meeting objectives. The days when all instructions from the boss were accepted without question are long gone. People want and expect more involvement (and explanation) than, "Because I said so" or "Because I'm in charge." Successful managers need to be able to persuade their own boss, the team, and colleagues.

LISTENING IS ACTIVE, NOT PASSIVE

We all like to believe we are good listeners. If this were true, there would be far fewer errors than there actually are. How often do you encounter situations in which an incorrect message has been received? For example, in a conversation with someone you are asked to do something. Later, it transpires that you have done something different from what was required. Where does the responsibility for the misunderstanding lie?

Certainly the "transmitter" must be clear, but the "receiver" also has a part to play in the communication process. Have you ever come out from a meeting and a colleague says, "I didn't understand a word of what so-and-so was saying"?

"Well, why didn't you ask, then?" you reply.

Your colleague answers, "I didn't want to look stupid."

Too many people see listening as keeping quiet and trying to concentrate on what is said and, what is more, view that as the safer option. How, then, can we listen better without missing the vital points?

Listening has to be an active process; as the receiver, we must become involved. Listening effectively has two facets: listening better and coping with embarrassment.

Following are some suggestions to help listen more effectively.

1. Ensure that you have understood the main point(s) by reflecting them back to the transmitter. For example, "Did you say that the meeting was moved to 3 pm, Marion?" This helps you to check that you have understood the message correctly.
2. Some people wrongly think they will look stupid if they do this. Actually, the reverse applies, provided it is not overdone. The transmitter generally sees it as showing interest and trying to understand.

As a manager, work toward developing an environment where questions from team members are encouraged and "there is no such thing as a stupid question." This will greatly reduce chances of miscommunication and misunderstandings.

SUMMARIZE AND ENCOURAGE QUESTIONS

Called upon to chair meetings, most people learn very quickly that occasional summaries are important for clarity and understanding. Unfortunately, this skill sometimes often fails to find its way into day-to-day communications. All too often, people try to impart extremely complex information without any summary of main points or opportunity for questions. Because they understand it, they assume that everyone else will.

The receiver can easily be made to feel as if everything is being done at full gallop when he would much prefer to trot. Interestingly, these high-speed communications often end with a question such as "You understand all that, don't you, John?"

What is John likely to reply? Few would have the courage to say "In fact you went so fast that I was totally lost after the first sentence. Would you give me an instant replay of the entire conversation please?"

The more complex the information, the more summaries you should make. Try to break the information down into chunks and summarize the main points—those points that must be understood and retained—at the end of each section. For example, a parent might spend five minutes or more explaining to his child how to cross the road safely, but he often summarizes with: "Remember, always look both ways before you step off the curb!" You might also want to disseminate written summaries of salient points through handouts, e-mail, or a visual aid, such as PowerPoint. Written communication is often the best way to supplement and reinforce oral discussion.

As mentioned in the previous section, you should also encourage questions that help understanding. Some people, however, need verbal support (not just a subtle prompt) to ask questions. For example, "I've covered a lot of ground here. Indeed I found it all rather confusing myself at first, so I would be surprised if you didn't a have few questions. I'd like to hear them."

DEFUSING VERBAL AGGRESSION AND INTERROGATION

Oral aggression can be defined as using personal attacks to get what you (or someone else) want. For example, "That's typical. Fine manager you are. Guys like me have to work on Saturday while you're off watching football. You're paid twice my salary and have no thought for anyone else but yourself." Handling this type of intimidation is hard! Some people seem to cope with it better than others, but no one finds it easy.

How would you respond to such aggression? Answers might be the following:

- "Don't be negative. Occasional weekend work is in your contract, if you bothered to look. And this is the time you're supposed to be doing it—oh, by the way, your merit raise is due next month!"

- "Right . . . Well, I suppose I had better find someone else to do it then."

The first response turns it into a full-blown confrontation, and nobody wins those. Even if you (the manager) are right, you have dropped to the other person's emotional level. It neither looks professional nor sends the right message. The second response will probably remove most, if not all, of the aggression. But what have you taught the aggressor? That bullying works! "If I shout loudly enough, I'll win." A better answer might be: "I understand how you feel, but this work needs to be done by the deadline. And you're the only one qualified who's responsible for this area. Plus, your contract does call for some work on weekends. But how about this? Let's look at your schedule and see what we can do about taking some time off, as long as you work the required number of hours per week." Although you are standing your ground, you're playing to the other person's sense of fairness and offering him something in return—in this case, a more flexible schedule within the constraints of his job—along with reinforcing the fact that you consider him a vital team member. Most people will respond to a logical approach that's seasoned with empathy.

Also, consider the source. Some people rarely become angry, and when they do, they are usually justified. If you make a mistake or unwittingly do something that makes someone justifiably upset, then apologize and do everything possible to correct the error.

When someone launches a personal attack, try asking *questions*. Questions have the effect of making the person stop and think instead of just reacting. Open-ended questions often help get to the bottom of the situation and help defuse the person's anger.

Watch Out for Machine-Gun Questions

On the other hand, when questions are "machine-gun," a rat-a-tat-tat series of queries that follow each other without a noticeable pause, they can backfire. For example, "Carlos, what has caused the delay with that project? Is it too much staff absence? What do you think we can do about it? Shall I authorize some overtime?" and so on. Poor old Carlos hasn't a chance either to think or answer. He's probably wondering, "Which question do you want me to answer?" The "easy" solution for most people is to reply to the last question!

People who ask "machine-gun" questions often do not realize they are doing it. Although the questioner is trying to help, they are too impatient to wait for an answer. Often in these circumstances a good open-ended question to collect information is immediately followed by one that suggests the answer (see above example). If you think you might be a "machine-gun inquisitor," discuss it with someone whose opinion you trust for their view.

If such is the case, ask questions one at a time and then pause after each question (silently count to three). This tack avoids the confusion engendered by machine-gun questioning. It gives the responder time to think, and enables the situation to be handled one step at a time. It might take a little longer to get answers, but the eventual outcome is far more effective and satisfactory.

CONSENSUS DECISION-MAKING VERSUS PERSUASION

Most managers are involved in decision-making with others. Sometimes the objective is to reach a decision in circumstances where no one favors any particular option at the outset and everyone is collectively trying to find the best solution (consensus decision-making, discussed in Chapter 6). On other occasions, the manager has a strong view about one of the options and wants to convince the others to take or reject this course of action (persuasion).

Unfortunately, it is all too easy to confuse the two approaches or not even consider them as separate. Such confusion can result in a less-than-effective solution being chosen—to keep people happy—because someone went along with it rather than being convinced. Conversely, if one person is trying to persuade in a situation where all of the others feel that an impartial (objective) analysis of all options is called for, the "persuader" may well be seen as unreasonably dominating.

Prior to any decision-making meeting, decide what role you need to play. If you and the others involved have no particular objective except to find an appropriate solution, then it is a *consensus*. The aim is to hear all views and collectively choose a solution that has been mutually developed by everyone. Another option is *compromise*, in which various factions give up something to come to a solution that everyone can live with.

If, however, you feel that a particular solution or option should be adopted or rejected, then you need to be in *persuasion* mode. Prepare your case thoroughly before the meeting: Emphasize the benefits of your proposal, and anticipate likely objections to it.

WHAT DO YOU WANT TO ACHIEVE WHEN PERSUADING?

Although the answer to this question may seem obvious, many times people are vague about exactly what they want when they attempt to persuade others. They have a general idea, but their plan lacks specifics.

For example, a manager needs some additional staff for a short period to complete an important project on time. The manager makes this request to her manager, and she is given two people for a week. At the end of that week, however, she goes back again asking for further help because the work is still not finished. What she needed in the first place—if she had done her homework properly—was three people for two weeks.

So it's important to be specific in your requests. Otherwise you may end up with something different from what you need.

Stating specifics at the outset can be a powerful tool to get what you need. For example, when Mary was promoted to management, she was offered a very low pay raise. Rather than accept it, she wrote a detailed description of what she believed her superior's expectations were of her and assigned a monetary value to those duties. She then approached company management with these expectations—all based on the work she was supposed to perform. As a result of stating specific requirements both in terms of duties and benefits, Mary received a pay raise five times the initial offer.

Before trying to persuade, decide the specific result that you want and communicate it very clearly to the other party. Otherwise, you may end up with something completely different, since the other person probably can't read your mind (nor you theirs).

SET LIMITS WHEN PERSUADING OR NEGOTIATING

On the other hand, some people set their minds on a very specific result then adopt an all-or-nothing approach when trying to persuade. For example:

> *Business owner (to bank manager):* "I need an advance of
> $2,000 for two months."
> *Bank manager:* "I can let you have $1,000 for one month."
> *Owner:* "It's two months or nothing."
> *Bank manager:* "Right. It's nothing then!"

That went well . . . not exactly! Negotiation is often—not always, but often—an integral part of persuasion. Room to maneuver is important. Some people, though, never allow themselves any wiggle room and end up in a situation similar to the business owner, paying a big price for their inflexibility. Effective persuaders and negotiators set limits—usually within which they are prepared to operate. This limit is set by a series of questions, such as:

- What is the best I can realistically hope to achieve? ($1,500 for two months)
- What would I be happy to achieve? ($2,000 for one month)

- What is the lower (or upper) limit beyond which I cannot go? ($750 for one month)

Note the word *realistically* in the first question. Going in with an unrealistic demand will generate animosity right from the start because the other person knows he stands no chance of closing the gap. So be honest with yourself about what can be achieved.

BOTTOM-LINE PEOPLE VERSUS DETAIL PEOPLE

Have you ever heard someone interrupt the middle of a presentation and say, "Just cut to the chase!" In effect, they are saying, "I don't need all this detail in order to respond." It may be impatience, but it could also be a compliment. "I know you have already done your homework, so give me the proposal." This is a "bottom-line" person in action.

Conversely, the presenter might be covering the main points only and be constantly interrupted with questions such as "How exactly did you arrive at that figure?" or "What risks have you considered?" It may be distrust but it is often caused by the questioner's need to verify that the I's have been dotted and the T's crossed to their satisfaction. This is a "detail" person.

When persuading, be aware of the needs of the person you are trying to convince. Otherwise you may not get what you want. Prepare thoroughly, irrespective of how much information you intend to impart. Before going into the meeting, ask yourself whether you are dealing with a "bottom-line" person or a "detail" person:

- If it's a "bottom-line" person, give her the meat of your proposal right at the start along with the chief benefits. Then ask her if she needs further information and be prepared to provide her with details if need be.
- If it's a "detail" person, explain the process you used to arrive at a proposal and ask which areas he would like you to cover in

detail. Sometimes he only wants a summary, so be prepared to do that.

Either way, expect to answer questions and provide as much information as you can. What you're doing is "packaging"—tailoring your arguments to meet the needs of the decision-maker.

A WIN/WIN APPROACH IS BETTER THAN WIN/LOSE

Persuasion (and negotiation) is seen by some as a form of competitive sport. "I need to win this one, and if that means beating the opposition into submission, so be it!" These people have the mistaken impression that in order to win, their opponents must lose. The main difficulty with this approach is the aftermath. You might win the battle but lose the war because of the bad feeling your action has generated. Rather than turning the other cheek some people prefer to do repaying of their own when the opportunity presents itself. And you know what they say about payback.

With a win/win approach, however, you endeavor to ensure that both parties gain something. In a sense, it's a modern form of horse trading. You might try for the bigger, faster, cheaper horse, but, in the end, the other party still receives some reward. Nothing is gained if you shoot your opponent's horse! With win/win, both parties leave the discussion feeling that they have gained something. One might gain more than the other, but there is progress on both sides. Go into any negotiation with a suggestion as to what the person you hope to persuade can gain. By offering him a carrot you just might get a better horse!

ALWAYS LEAVE THE DOOR OPEN

Occasionally you may find yourself in a straightforward situation that demands a "yes" or "no," or a "do it" or "don't do it" outcome.

The other party either accepts your decision or not. There is no room for any form of compromise. In cases like this ask, "How can I bring about a win/win result here?"

The outcome may have to be a firm decision one way or the other, but that doesn't mean one person must lose everything. Our egos are very fragile. If we are seen by others as having failed, we don't usually feel great about ourselves. How do you adopt a win/win approach in a straightforward decision situation without compromising your own position and objectives?

The answer is simple: Never push people into a corner without providing a doorway. A doorway allows people to save face when they have lost in this type of straightforward situation. Some examples of these doorways might include:

- Enabling them to gain something unrelated to the issue under discussion.
- Offering support by explaining an unpopular decision to their team.
- Accepting a proposal from them that would prevent a similar unpopular decision in the future.

For example, sometimes during hiring negotiations, the prospective employee will request a higher salary than the company can afford. The manager can offer additional vacation time to provide the needed doorway.

Before you meet, consider possible doorways that will provide future opportunities should this particular situation not work out.

TACTFUL HONESTY IS THE BEST POLICY

Some people modify the truth when trying to persuade and even when communicating generally. They seem to have little trust in people and then wonder why they are accorded so little trust and respect themselves.

Most people, when asked what they look for in a manager, usually put "Inspires respect and trust" among the most desirable characteristics. The most effective way to earn respect and trust is by being honest.

Modifying the truth might win some skirmishes, but ultimately it will lose the campaign. Sooner or later, people find out the truth. Once trust is compromised it is difficult, if not impossible, to regain.

Honesty does not mean telling everyone everything—but it means that what you do say is the truth. You cannot impart information given to you in confidence, but you can explain why you cannot discuss it.

When trying to persuade, tell people *precisely* what you want. Some would-be persuaders don't do this as they mistakenly think that they may gain more by being vague. This is rarely the case!

Honesty Works Well the Rest of the Time

What good does it do to tell someone that what he has done is fine and then go and complain about it to someone else? Eventually word will likely get back to the offended party. You will have lost his trust and caused resentment. Plus, by talking about that person behind his back, you'll likely lose credibility with the rest of your team ("The boss did it to Joe, so he'll probably do it to me!").

As a manager, it's your responsibility to be honest yet tactful. Address your concerns by talking directly to the person responsible about how you feel. You can tell the truth and still protect his feelings.

Tact does not always come naturally. It's a learned skill best cultivated by thinking before you speak. Simply put, tact is application of the Golden Rule: Treat others as you yourself would like to be treated. You have feelings, and so do other people. Active listening and encouraging questions discussed earlier in this chapter will also help develop sensitivity toward others.

Someone once said that diplomacy was the art of telling someone to go to hell in such a way that he looks forward to the trip. You'll never know when you'll need that person's help. So if you have a choice between hurting someone and being kind, choose kindness.

TAKE-AWAY POINTS

- Despite advances in modern technology, oral communication and persuasion continue to be important.
- Effective listening is an active process that requires communication skills and the willingness to ask pertinent questions.
- Respond to verbal aggression by using logic and, again, asking questions. Not only will the latter help you get to the bottom of and defuse the situation, but it may result in solutions.
- Recognize the difference between getting consensus and persuasion. If the latter is required, be specific about what you want and when.
- In negotiation, allow for wiggle room and compromise. Even if it's a "yes or no" answer, enable the other person to save face by giving her something.
- When persuading, pay attention to the needs of your audience—are they detail or bottom-line? Tailor your arguments accordingly and have additional information.
- Although honesty is the best policy, it should be leavened with tact.

CHAPTER 8

Teamwork and Coaching

CHAPTER OBJECTIVES

To understand what coaching, leadership, and motivation mean

To recognize why they are important and how different aspects can be used in management

To define principles to help you coach, as well as lead and motivate

To understand the importance of mentoring

INTRODUCTION

Encouraging your team to achieve its goals is a challenge for any manager, regardless of level of experience. Approaches vary enormously from person to person and situation to situation.

Effective guidance relies on three factors: coaching, leadership, and motivation. The purpose of this chapter is to define each and provide basic guidelines as to how these factors can achieve results. Each person will probably approach a given situation in a slightly different way—and that is as it should be.

Rather than being clear-cut and distinct, these factors are more or less intertwined, so you may be doing all three simultaneously. Or you may use certain aspects of one or the other to reach your goals. Often the most effective plans draw from the various strategies to suit whatever fits the situation.

Managers should also take time to mentor. Along with providing a sense of continuity, you have the reward of helping someone along with their career and passing along your knowledge and expertise.

COACHING, LEADERSHIP, AND MOTIVATION

Managing for Excellence[13] defines *coaching* as "the art of improving the performance of others." For managers, this means encouraging team members to learn from and be challenged by their work, as well as creating conditions for continuous development by helping staff define and achieve goals.

In contrast, *leadership* involves knowing what is required and using the right approach—appropriate for both the circumstances and the people involved—to enable the team to gain its objective. At some point in our careers, most of us have used the wrong approach and paid the price for it! But the right approach in leadership can yield amazing results. Author Stephen Covey[14] differentiates between a *manager* and a *leader.* When on a trek through the jungle, he hypothesizes, the manager can follow the map, but the leader is the one who climbs the palm tree and discovers the best route.

However, if you ask twenty people to define motivation, you are likely to receive as many different answers. Some people feel that the only true motivation comes from within, fueled by inspiration or the desire to succeed. Nevertheless, the manager can certainly help. In this context, *motivation* is best defined as the desire to accomplish a goal or participate in an endeavor.

While not always the case, there does seem to be a correlation between motivation and results. A motivated person usually achieves results or, put another way, achievement usually motivates.

WHY COACH?

Recently, coaching has become widespread in management and in many cases has replaced counseling, which can imply that the employee falls short of the company's standard (hence the need for counseling) and is in some manner being penalized and reprimanded (if only in the nicest way). Coaching offers a more positive and encouraging approach. It levels the playing field and provides an opportunity to ask open-ended questions and discover solutions mutually beneficial to all parties.

According to corporate coach Beth Agnew the coachee (person being coached) "can find solutions consistent with their values and capabilities, thus improving performance."[15] Other benefits include developing competence and confidence, easier diagnosis of problems in behavior and performance, and maintaining the dignity of team members. Coaching can also foster better working relationships in the group "as employees begin to coach each other." By being coached, team members:

- Have a comfortable environment in which to vent and express their feelings
- Develop skills that are already in place
- Learn new skills
- Gain insight into themselves and colleagues
- Get unbiased support
- Gain fresh perspectives on issues
- Get advice, suggestions, and options[16]

The downside of coaching is that it can take an inordinate amount of time, and when frustrated, managers may find themselves reverting to the "counseling or authoritative style" of management, cautions Agnew. Because of the "supervisor/subordinate relationship [of managers and employees], a true level and equal coaching stance can never be fully achieved."

USING COACHING TO BUILD A GOOD TEAM

Nevertheless, coaching can be used in many management and team-building situations, particularly when you're starting out as a manager or working with a new group of employees. Early on, it sets the stage for performance and allows for rules that apply to everyone in the group, creating an atmosphere of fairness and, in some cases, healthy competition.

Managing for Excellence[17] offers a model of six basic stages for each goal that you're trying to achieve when coaching:

1. **Definition:** Determine performance goals (coach/ coachee(s) must agree on goals)

2. **Analysis:** Define the current reality (What is the present position?)
3. **Exploration:** Look at various options that will achieve goals
4. **Action:** What tasks are needed to achieve goals (involves a commitment by all parties)

These four stages can sometimes be accomplished in a single coaching session. From there, the coachee goes on to the next steps:

5. **Learning:** The coachee implements the agreed-upon action with the support of the coach (this can take considerable time, depending upon the goal or desired performance)
6. **Feedback:** Review progress, determine what has been learned, and how the coachee can build upon this knowledge to reach the next goal

Effective coaching not only helps develop the skills and talents of each team member, but it gives the program momentum and offers a definable benchmark for goals as well as opportunities to set new goals. However, it does require effort on the part of the managers who will need to keep a positive attitude and set aside time for coaching, encourage team members to come up with new ideas and take responsibility for same, and offer support and resources to achieve various goals.

SET A SOLID COURSE FOR YOUR TEAM

Some managers seem to view leadership as simply providing day-to-day direction for the team and dealing with the everyday problems that arise. While this aspect is important, it tends to make life static, and the emphasis swings toward maintaining the status quo. Nothing changes, moves forward, or improves.

A manager of an Accounts department (with an enormous outstanding debt from invoices owing for over 120 days) was once heard to remark to a director: "Well, we do receive the money invoiced eventually, don't we?"

The director replied: "True, but shouldn't you be looking at ways of ensuring quicker payment of our invoices? Otherwise there might not possibly be enough in the bank to pay your salary next month!"

Unlike the aforementioned Accounts manager, the best leaders have a clear vision of the future, which represents an improvement over the present. Consider the following possibilities:

- Look at your principal objectives and ask yourself if they do, or should, represent an improvement over where you are now.
- How about that good idea you've had sitting in the back of your mind but so far have done nothing with? Try turning it into an objective for yourself and your team.
- Ask yourself and your team: "What should the department be doing in one or two years' time, and what should we be doing now to get there?"

WHEN ACCEPTANCE IS AS GOOD AS COMMITMENT . . .

"Commitment" can be defined as, "I want to do it," whereas "acceptance" is, "I have to do it." Some managers seem to set themselves the unreasonable target of gaining commitment from their team on everything!

Have you ever sat through a one-and-a-half-hour meeting at which you were asked for your views on some issue only to be told at the end that the board had already made the decision? Irritating, isn't it? The manager wanted to appear democratic but in reality was being autocratic. Consider the circumstances you are facing, and ask yourself whether you require commitment or just acceptance from your people. Some managerial decisions are bound to be unpopular. Suppose the board decides that in order to save money and jobs it is necessary for everyone with a company car to downgrade it on the next change. Probably nobody is going to welcome that idea, and the likelihood of gaining commitment is zero! Acceptance, though, is feasible if the situation is properly explained and the reasons given—but don't expect people to like it! The reverse, of course, is also true. Mere "acceptance" won't work if what you need is true "commitment."

EXCEPT WHEN YOU REALLY NEED COMMITMENT

In the previous section, we defined commitment as "I want to do it" and acceptance as "I have to do it." Being content with simple acceptance when commitment is needed is dangerous, to say the least. Acceptance means that the person feels he or she has no choice except to do whatever is required but is likely to do only the absolute minimum.

A salesperson was told to sell five products on behalf of another sales team to enable them to meet their monthly target. He sold the five required and no more, even though the opportunity to sell more was there if he had taken it . . . and he knew it! Had his manager originally asked for and gained his commitment, the salesperson would likely have sold more items—but then the manager never found out about the ignored opportunity.

Commitment usually—but not inevitably—equals involvement. Commitment through involvement means asking for the person's views and feelings and being prepared to discuss them in order to arrive at a suitable outcome. However, make sure that you separate open from closed questions here. Open questions get information and are more useful, whereas closed questions just produce yes or no answers. For example:

- How do you think we should tackle it? (Open question)
- You will do that, won't you? (Closed question)

Commitment without much involvement may well be possible if the person sees you as the expert in that situation and is happy to trust your judgment. For example, say you ask a team member to help resolve a problem with a customer. The team member is unfamiliar with the situation, so you give him general instructions as to how to handle it. The implicit agreement is that you know what you're doing and that the team member trusts you enough to follow your advice in dealing with the issue.

WHEN "I DON'T KNOW" IS THE RIGHT ANSWER

When first promoted to a management job, people are usually very aware of the need to earn the respect of the teams they now manage. They believe that, as managers, they should have all the answers that the teams need to do their various jobs effectively; otherwise, the team members will not respect them. Many new managers are afraid that if they say they don't know, they will lose credibility.

But this fear of admitting we don't know causes even more difficulties and can generate problems:

- The manager guesses (incorrectly and without admitting it) at an answer. As a result, the team believes the information to be true when it is not, and the team's subsequent actions are also wrong.
- The manager waffles, the team recognizes the indecision, and the manager's credibility suffers.
- Because of inadequate background information, the manager makes inappropriate decisions about possible actions.

As a rule of thumb, it takes three to six months for a new manager to realize that her team does not expect her to have all the answers. So be assured that there is no loss of credibility in occasionally saying:

- "I don't know, but I will find out!"
- "I'm not sure which is the best way to proceed. What do you think?"

This approach increases rather than diminishes credibility, provided it is not done constantly.

KEEP IT POSITIVE, EVEN WHEN CHALLENGED

Unfortunately, some managers appear to treat any form of disagreement as a personal insult, considering it a lack of respect or a challenge to their authority.

Often such managers attack the person who is disagreeing. "Don't question my decisions, Jane. I have made the decision. Your job is simply to do it!" Not surprisingly, this kind of rebuke often has damaging consequences for the team member's motivation.

Few people enjoy negative reactions. However, as a manager it's important to look at the reason *why* the team member is disagreeing with you. Consider these three negative responses from team members:

1. "I am concerned there won't be time to do that by deadline." This statement gives the reason for disagreement and indicates a valid problem. You should treat it constructively and find a solution or compromise together.
2. "It won't work—we tried that before." No details are given in this statement. You should therefore concentrate on finding out more about the last time this action was attempted and see if there's a solution.
3. "Sometimes you think you only have to speak and everyone else has to jump five feet in the air. You can't insist that I work on the weekend." In this situation, the employee is lashing out. Although it can be construed as a personal attack and the instinctive reaction is to respond in kind,

you will gain nothing and in fact will likely make things worse. Cool the situation down by asking the person to explain why he feels as he does. Only then can you logically deal with his reasons. Remember, he may have a point, albeit badly put, and perhaps you are wrong.

Each of the above statements presents a vastly different reaction, although some people respond equally strongly to all three because they are all negative. So try to differentiate between them and to get to the cause of the problem or negative reaction.

AVOID THE "PROVIDE GOODIES" TRAP

In a sense, the "provide goodies" trap is a form of bribery. For example, if there is a tough or unpopular job to be done, some managers think that they must resort to managerial enticement. Thus, for example, the manager says: "Carlos, I know you will need to work late this week to meet this new deadline. But if you do it, then you can take your partner out for a meal at the company's expense over the weekend."

At first glance, you might think: "What on earth is wrong with that? At least the manager is showing appreciation." Some team members may well see it that way, but others might see it as special treatment for Carlos and could even be offended by it. Secondly, what is Carlos likely to expect if asked to work late in the future?

Instead, use recognition; that is, show your thanks and appreciation after the event. Material rewards are not always necessary. People don't usually do things for material rewards all of the time. Most of us have done things because we want to help others. Often a sincere "Thanks for what you did" is sufficient when well and sincerely put.

If you feel some action beyond the call of duty warrants a more tangible form of recognition, consider springing it as a surprise afterward, and only do so when it is justified. Also remember that reward or recognition should be meaningful to the employee. For instance, if an employee has several young children, tickets to a family-themed park might be appropriate. Such actions should be very occasional. If special gestures of appreciation become the norm, they will thereafter be expected by all employees.

Recognition is a very powerful motivator. "Providing goodies," however, can offend and be counterproductive.

BE PREPARED TO MAKE A DECISION

Often, actually analyzing the pros and cons of the various options is not too difficult. Saying, "We will choose that one" can be the hard task. Unfortunately, some managers seem to make a career out of being indecisive and sitting on the fence. Whenever they are asked for a decision, they ask for more information or say that they need to think about it then end up doing nothing. For a team member who does not have the necessary authority to decide, this is one of the most frustrating situations imaginable.

For instance, John says to his manager, "Marion, you need to decide if XYZ Ltd can have a 20 percent discount on this order for $2 million by five o'clock today, otherwise they are likely to buy elsewhere."

"Leave it with me, John. I'll have to think about it," and off goes Marion to a meeting.

Five o'clock comes and . . . nothing! Next day John checks with XYZ—the order is lost! Why? The manager failed to make a decision when it was needed. You do not want to be that manager!

Of course, under certain circumstances (not the above!) not deciding can be the right thing to do (see "You Will Never Have All of the Information. Decide!" on page 75). If you need time to weigh the facts, find out if there is any deadline for the decision and explain why you need some time. And make sure that you respond when needed, if not before.

You might also consider whether it is appropriate to delegate authority (with limits) to the team member for future decisions of this type. If that course of action is feasible, everyone may save time and motivation is increased as well.

ASK THE RIGHT QUESTIONS TO MOTIVATE YOUR TEAM

Most managers accept that motivation is important. However, sometimes managers make assumptions about what they believe motivates their team members. These assumptions are often based on the manager's own values, which may be nowhere near those of the individual concerned.

A common assumption is "Everyone wants a promotion. Therefore something to provide progress toward this goal will motivate." Wrong! Not everyone desires the responsibility that goes with promotion, and pushing extra responsibility at them might in fact put a damper on their enthusiasm.

Other managers realize the danger of assumptions and therefore ask: "What motivates you, Anton?" This is a very hard and complex question, and, not surprisingly, people tend to give simple off-the-cuff answers: "I could do with more money" or "A new car would be nice."

Few managers can provide such immediate material rewards, which would only result in short-term motivation anyway. A better question might be: "What do you enjoy doing, Anton?" There will probably be a pause as Anton thinks this one through.

Anton's answers will relate to the work itself and therefore give you a far better picture of what actually motivates him. You'll get an idea of what his enthusiasms are and what areas he feels he can excel in. You can then plan together how you might apply some or all of the information to his workload and the team goals in the future.

GENUINE PRAISE IS A POWERFUL MOTIVATOR

The philosophy in business that underlies the actions of some managers is "If you are doing something wrong, I will talk to you about it. If things are going well, I will leave you alone." Consequently, team members may warn new members joining the team: "Don't expect any thanks from the manager, but if you make a mistake, you'll soon hear about it!"

Unfortunately, some managers who adopt this philosophy don't even realize they are doing so, but members of their team certainly recognize it! Other managers deliberately refrain from praising employees because they fear it will be seen as idle flattery and have little effect (or even have a negative effect, in that the employee might become complacent and not work as hard).

The problems associated with the "no news is good news" approach are twofold:

- Any time the manager calls someone into the office to talk, that team member's shoulders immediately slump. "What have I done wrong now?" is the initial reaction.
- Everyone has their own unique strengths and weaknesses, but this approach misses the opportunity to reinforce the strengths. Those strengths may even decay in the struggle to correct weaknesses.

Managers must praise a job well done as well as correct matters when things are done improperly. Most people want objective, balanced feedback from their manager, and genuine praise is an important part of that. "Praise" means recognition backed up by hard fact.

For example: "I thought your meeting went very well. The objectives were clear to all. You turned Mike's disagreements into something positive, and all of our objectives for it were met. Good job!" And then perhaps a solicitation for feedback: "Can you share what you learned and how you accomplished it?"

SOME ARE MORE MOTIVATED THAN OTHERS

Do you consider yourself highly motivated? Most managers (or aspiring managers) believe that they are well motivated, otherwise they would not be effective in their jobs. There are exceptions, but only a few!

If a manager is motivated and giving her best most of the time, she probably expects everyone on her team to do likewise. She may have trouble grasping why some people do not seem to respond to a set of circumstances the way she herself does. She tries everything she can think of to create a positive reaction, or at least some slight show of enthusiasm, but without success. While her intention is laudable, without figuring out what motivates her employees, she is expecting the impossible.

As mentioned before, don't make assumptions. Find out how people feel. Accept that some people will never be as highly motivated as you. They are happy to do the job adequately for which they are paid, go home, and forget about it. If they are content doing that, who is to say that anything is wrong? Not everyone wants extra responsibility, promotion, and so on.

Put your motivational efforts into those who will respond, and maintain the current motivational level of those who can't or don't wish to go further. It is a realistic way of dealing with a variety of people and their different approaches.

THE IMPORTANCE OF MENTORING

A *mentor* is someone who shares his knowledge, wisdom, and experience about his occupation or workplace. You may have had the fortunate experience of having one or more mentors during various stages of your career.

Mentors are different from coaches (discussed earlier in this chapter) in that it's a much more personal relationship. You've found someone (perhaps a younger, less experienced version of yourself) whom you feel holds great promise. So you want to help him along. Seeing him grow and develop professionally can be gratifying and rewarding to both of you. Mentoring also challenges your management style and helps you refine it as you teach it to others.

According to the Small Business Administration (SBA),[18] mentors should do the following:

- Provide guidance based on past business experiences.
- Create a positive counseling relationship and climate of open communication.
- Help the protégé ("mentee") identify problems and solutions.
- Lead the protégé through the problem-solving processes.
- Offer constructive criticism in a supportive way.
- Share stories, including mistakes.
- Assign "homework" if applicable.
- Refer the protégé to other business associates.
- Be honest about business expertise.
- Solicit feedback from the protégé.
- Come prepared to discuss issues.

The SBA also recommends being clear about how and when you'll help and understanding that the relationship will end (or take a different form) when the mentee moves on. At some point the mentee may resist your suggestions, and the relationship may encounter difficulties as you provide honest feedback. Mentors can only offer counseling to a point—the protégé needs to find his own path.

TAKE-AWAY POINTS

- Because it focuses on solutions in a positive, reinforcing environment, coaching has replaced counseling in many management situations. It is also used in team building and goal setting.

- Leadership is important in setting a solid course for your team as well as developing new ideas.
- Recognize the difference between acceptance and commitment. It's unrealistic to expect employees to commit to every idea or action. Similarly understand that not all team members are equally motivated; some may just want to do the job and nothing more.
- Rather than assuming that everyone is motivated by the same things, ask specific questions to discern what drives members of your team.
- Admitting "I don't know" is perfectly fine, especially during your first few months as a manager. However, avoid making it a constant or habitual answer. The same is true for making decisions. They should be made on time, within deadlines. Better yet, if you can and it's feasible, delegate that decision to the responsible team member.
- If you get a negative response from a team member, listen to what the person is saying. Even if it seems to be a personal attack, try to find out the underlying reasons for the employee's dissatisfaction.
- Avoid "providing goodies" (bribes) for unpopular or tedious tasks but do offer recognition and praise for a job well done. Take an even-handed approach when dealing with team members, interspersing constructive criticism with positive reinforcement.
- Take time to mentor. One of the most rewarding aspects of managing is being able to help individuals, whether it be coaching and guiding your team or nurturing someone you feel has a special talent in your area of expertise or workplace.

CHAPTER 9

How to Delegate

CHAPTER OBJECTIVES

To comprehend the purpose, meaning, and importance of delegation

To learn to delegate effectively

INTRODUCTION

Delegation is probably one of the hardest skills for a manager to learn. The uppermost feeling is often: "If I delegate, things will be out of my control. I don't want a failure, so I'll do it myself." This results in a closed loop, and an overburdened manager! Fear is the main barrier to delegation. Yet good—that is, effective—delegation means that the task is under (as opposed to being out of) control.

DELEGATION AND WHY IT IS IMPORTANT

Delegation is entrusting part of your job as a manager (specific activities or decisions) to a member of your team and giving them the responsibility and authority to carry it out. However, as a manager you, rather than the employee, are ultimately accountable and answerable for the activity. The act of delegation must be separated from simply issuing work. *Issuing work* means deciding which member of the team should carry out some task that is part of their normal role anyway. Delegation, on the other hand, involves giving someone a task that is normally part of the manager's job.

Effective delegation is important for the following reasons:

- It enables the manager to spend time on more important tasks.
- It's an excellent way of developing people who wish to advance in the organization.
- It is highly motivational—although, if done badly, the reverse can also be true.

PICK THE RIGHT TASK

Some managers believe they are delegating when in fact all they are doing is issuing work that would normally be done by a member of the team anyway.

Others consider delegating part of their job, but then the only tasks that seem to be delegated are those that the manager can't be bothered to do personally. Still other managers only delegate when they are in "work overload," as in, "Mavis, would you finish off the figures on my monthly report for me? I have to go to that section meeting now and won't have time to do them."

To delegate effectively, determine which tasks to select. Make an initial list of all the main tasks you perform. Then ask yourself which would be worth delegating for the following reasons:

- It would save you valuable time.
- It might motivate a member of the team.
- It would help develop someone's skills and/or knowledge.

Now that you have identified those tasks that you could delegate, you need to find the right person to delegate to.

PICK THE RIGHT PERSON

You can probably think of at least one member of your team whom you would immediately consider as a prime candidate. Such people are usually experienced and need little briefing from you. Plus, they offer to help in a crisis. Every manager needs—or would like—someone like that on her team. The danger is that such a person will take on too much. Some managers never consider delegating anything to an inexperienced or new member of the team because they assume, perhaps subconsciously, that no experience signifies a lack of ability. How, then, do you go about choosing the right person for the task?

First, ask yourself *why* you are considering delegating this particular task. Now think about the skill and knowledge requirements of the task and the individual strengths and needs of the people on your team in this particular field (previous discussion at appraisal or review meetings should help here).

Next, try to match the task requirements to the individual strengths and needs. Remember, do not assume lack of experience means no ability—sometimes someone with less experience takes a fresh approach to the job and can do it even more efficiently. And also consider how the added work will affect the productivity and schedule of the trusted team member.

Once you feel you've chosen the right person, set a specific objective: for example, "Develop Andrew's financial control skills and knowledge within three months by delegating production of the monthly 'budget versus spend' report to him."

PICK THE RIGHT CHALLENGE

Make sure your perception of a challenge is commensurate with that of your team members. Consider the following example:

Karen (the manager): "Dawn, I need your help. I've just been told that I'm going on a management course next week and we've got to purchase some additional computers. I was scheduled to put together a proposal and discuss it with the director. Since I'm going away, and you're my right-hand person, I'd like you to take a crack at it."

Dawn (the assistant, trying to keep the panic out of her voice): "Thanks for thinking of me, Karen, but I have never put a proposal together, much less tried to persuade a director with one! I'm not at all sure that I could do that . . . I have no idea how to prepare a presentation, let alone give one."

Karen: "Everyone has to start somewhere. I had to do that sort of thing when I was in your position eighteen months ago.

My predecessor used to believe in throwing people in at the deep end, and that's how I learned. This will be a good challenge for you. There's nothing like a meeting with a director to focus the mind. I'm sure you'll cope if you give it a try."

Dawn (anxious to leave the office because she wants to find a more experienced team member to help bail her out): "Well, I sincerely doubt it . . . and you won't even be here to provide guidance."

How do you think Dawn will fare? What is seen by Karen as a challenge is seen by Dawn as impossible. Because you can do something (or could when you were in a team member's job) does not mean someone else can. As discussed in previous chapters, everyone has different abilities, goals, and talents.

Before deciding to delegate a task to a particular team member, ask yourself if he has (or can develop, in the time available) the knowledge and/or skills, as well as the confidence, to cope with the task. If you are unsure, you might want to sit down and discuss the possibility with him, to discern how he feels about it. Alternatively, you might want the potential delegatee to "ride shotgun" with you before formally handing over responsibility. Leaving the employee in charge when you're out for a day allows for a trial run. If after that, the team member still sees the task as impossible, consider giving the task to someone else.

TRUST PEOPLE—GIVE THEM THE AUTHORITY THEY NEED

Some managers seem altogether too happy to delegate responsibility to team members but never give them the authority to do the job properly. In this context, *authority* is defined as the power to make independent decisions. As mentioned earlier, failure to delegate effectively probably stems from fear. However, it is extremely frustrating to keep running to the manager every time a decision on even the most minor aspects of a delegated job is needed.

So how do you delegate the authority without relinquishing control or abdicating responsibility altogether? The answer is simple: allow the team member to make independent decisions within certain limitations. Setting limits will help avoid disasters.

For example, suppose you delegate the task of negotiating a price with an important customer. The team member will probably ask: "How far can I go?" to which you might reply: "We have quoted $90,000 for one module. Now they may find they need two and therefore want to negotiate. You can negotiate a discount of up to 10 percent—that gives a minimum price of $178,200 for two modules—or a lower discount and free maintenance worth $3,000, whichever you think most appropriate at the time. If they insist on a deal that would take us below the minimum price of $178,200, check with me before agreeing to anything."

This allows the team member some leeway for decision-making but prevents him from making costly—and serious—mistakes.

WHEN BORING TASKS ARE JUST THAT

Following is an example of what sometimes happens when a manager wants to "dress up" an otherwise boring task. The manager will say: "Something important has cropped up, Ann, which I think you will find interesting. The board wants an analysis of our sales over the last year by product and geographical district. As my assistant, you will have to prepare analyses one day, so how about starting now?"

What the manager means, however, is this: "Ann, I'm strapped for time, and our director is screaming for information. For the next couple of hours, I'll call out figures, and you punch the calculator and feed me the answers. By the way, I haven't the time to actually explain any of it at the moment!"

Not only do many managers make a habit of this deceptive approach, but they also think their victims actually believe what they tell them! Of course, the victim catches on quickly, so when the manager says he has "an interesting job," Ann knows that something boring or mundane is imminent. Sooner (usually) or later, people see through such deception, intentional or otherwise. So if you need a pair of eyes, arms, or legs to help with a boring but necessary task, say so up front. If you balance it out by delegating interesting and challenging work, most team members will be willing to help with even the most routine jobs.

ENCOURAGE PEOPLE TO DO THE PLANNING!

Some managers believe delegation involves telling team members what is required, exactly how it should be carried out, and by when. They usually offer the following rationale:

1. "Well, I've done it so many times and know the best way."
2. "They don't know how to do the job."

However, these are incorrect assumptions. Say you've done a task many times. Does that mean you know the best, or the only way of doing it? Of course not. Sometimes the person who tackles the job for the first time comes up with a new method that is more effective than what had been used for months or even years before.

Whatever the task, a plan is needed (even if fairly brief) to show who needs to do what and by when. Rather than suggest the plan, ask your team members how they would tackle the task. Then decide whether their method would achieve the objective. If it will work, let them do it their way, for they will be more committed to their course of action. Provide advice only if a basic flaw appears in their plan or if they have no idea how to go about the task.

ENCOURAGE PEOPLE TO CHECK IN, AND GIVE THEM ACCESS

When considering whether to delegate a task, managers sometimes fear that they will lose control. They think, "If I delegate this task, I'm not doing it, so I'm not in control of it." Attempting to overcome this perceived difficulty, the manager sets up frequent review dates to meet and see how things are going, then wonders why the team member does not show up for some of these meetings. The manager starts to develop delegator's twitch.

Suddenly the manager is constantly looking over the team member's shoulder, asking how things are going. Rather than finding this helpful or supportive, the team member usually sees this, often correctly, as interference or distrust.

So how do you maintain some control without interfering or showing distrust of the person to whom you have delegated the work? First, encourage the employee to suggest checkpoints—that is, the stages in the task when you should step in and do a quick review. She will likely come up with the same points as you, but now it's her brainchild, not your interference. Second, allow her access to you if she wants to discuss any aspects of the task: "I have given you the job because I know you can do it. Rather than have me constantly check on you, if you want to discuss anything, just come and talk to me." She now knows that she can get any information she wants at any time and has been given the impetus to do so.

EVERYONE MAKES MISTAKES WHEN THEY'RE LEARNING

Delegation can be rather like learning to drive, involving several near-misses: horrible crunching of gears, stalling at traffic lights, forgetting to signal occasionally, and so on. Gradually you become proficient and more skilled and experienced.

Very few people have the knack of doing an unfamiliar job perfectly the first time. Most managers realize this, and so to help, they are very specific about what they want and exactly how it must be done. There is of course sometimes a good reason for doing this, but if the objective is to help the person develop, she requires room to maneuver and be allowed the few mistakes that are inevitable as she learns.

However, some managers seem to expect perfection right from the start and tell the employee: "Do it my way exactly so that you won't make any mistakes and let me down." What sort of learning experience or development is that? The team member will hardly be able to think for herself when she must eventually make her own decisions. The situation is similar to a "helicopter parent" who hovers over his child, doing her homework and micromanaging her life, until the kid goes to college and is unable to function independently (and possibly flunks out or develops behavior problems).

So be prepared to accept a few minor mistakes while the team member develops skill and knowledge. At strategic points, jointly review her performance to find out what she has learned and what she would do differently next time.

A final note: During the discussion when you are jointly planning the task, try to anticipate and prevent any serious problems (potential disasters). Agree what actions are needed, and together work out the most effective way of monitoring them.

REALITY CHECK—HOW DO THEY FEEL ABOUT THE TASK?

Oftentimes managers neglect a very important aspect of delegation: They fail to find out how the team member *really* feels about doing the task. Some managers describe the task, and what is involved in its successful completion, in great detail, believing that a clear explanation is all that is necessary—that is, if you fully understand it, you will be prepared to do it. Their closing remark is usually "Do you understand all that?" What is the team member supposed to say? The answer is likely to be a vague nod or a mumbled "S'pose so." The manager believes everything is fine. The team member might well understand the task, but that does not mean that he wants to do it.

Successful delegation requires the team member's commitment and motivation, and the only real way to discern that is by asking directly. Many times managers seem to rely on mental brain waves or "vibes." While some managers are certainly good at discerning team members' attitudes, the chief danger is that "vibes" can be easily misinterpreted.

So in addition to explaining or discussing the task, toward the end of your conversation ask the team member how he feels about doing the task, and listen carefully to his answer. If he appears unhappy or uneasy about your instructions or his own role, find out why. Then you and the team member can work together in dealing with the concerns.

AVOID THE BLACK HOLE—GIVE FEEDBACK WHEN IT'S DONE

Most managers monitor progress on the delegated task as it proceeds. However, once the task has been completed, a strange phenomenon seems to rear its head—the "black hole."

The task (an important report, say) is delegated effectively, the team member is happy to do the work, and preparation of the report proceeds as planned with regular review discussions (praise for things done well and constructive discussion about any difficulties). Eventually the report is completed successfully and left on the boss's desk. Then what? Often, absolutely nothing! The report disappears into a "black hole" never to be seen or mentioned again.

Delegation should be a learning experience, and the most valuable learning comes from reviewing the outcome of a project after it has been completed. Yet, while there is feedback and discussion during the course of the project, a review discussion "after the fact" is extremely rare. Thus a key opportunity for positive learning—and future motivation—has been missed.

After completion of the task, agree on a date to sit down and review how the project went. Direct four questions (or your own version of them) to the team member and then discuss them:

1. How do you feel it went?
2. What went particularly well and why?

3. What difficulties did you encounter, and how did you handle them?
4. What have you learned, and how will you use the knowledge?

People like feedback if it is done constructively. The postmortem discussion should also contain a critique of the outcome as well as any feedback from superiors on content, and so forth. The discussion can be brief, and the resulting benefits will be more than worth the time spent.

TAKE-AWAY POINTS

- Pick the right task and person. This may not always be the most experienced team member but perhaps someone whose talent you want to help develop.
- Challenge, but make sure the team member has the confidence and ability to get the job done. If the team member seems unwilling or intimidated by the task, listen to and respect his or her desires.
- Trust people, and give them the authority they need. Allow them to make their own decisions (within limits) and plans rather than doing it your way. Thus they will have a sense of ownership and be more motivated.
- Define boring tasks as such up front, and balance them with challenging or interesting work. Most people are willing to help, especially if they're motivated and treated honestly.
- Encourage people to suggest checkpoints, and give them access to you. Accept that they will make mistakes while they are learning.
- After you've described and explained the task to the team member, ask him directly how he feels about doing it!
- Avoid the "black hole" of zero feedback—review the outcome after the task has been completed.

CHAPTER 10

Presenting Information and Proposals

CHAPTER OBJECTIVES

To understand the difference between presenting information and proposals

To learn how and why to effectively present ideas

To define some principles to help you to present your ideas effectively

INTRODUCTION

The prospect of having to present information or make proposals to others in the organization usually makes the adrenalin flow. That's not always a good thing. Even normally self-confident managers find themselves undergoing panic attacks and discover they have contracted the "What if. . . ?" syndrome, the symptoms of which include:

- "What if I freeze and can't remember anything?"
- "What if I talk too fast?"
- "What if I can't answer their questions?"
- "What if they reject my ideas?"

This chapter contains some ideas to help combat "What if-itis" and its symptoms.

THE IMPORTANCE OF EFFECTIVE PRESENTATIONS

Presenting means formally imparting information, opinions, and/or ideas to others so that they are not only heard but also understood. Presenting *proposals* goes one step further by adding the element of persuasion in a formal situation (usually to a group).

As a manager, your ability to effectively impart information to groups is vital. It's a way of getting across your message and being understood. We have all sat through a poor presentation at some time or another. How much did you absorb? Your recommendations will only be accepted—which is the whole point of the exercise—if you are able to present your proposal effectively.

NERVES ARE NORMAL

Before giving a presentation, you'll likely have some form of stage fright ("nerves"). Typical symptoms include:

- Heart pumping
- Damp/shaking hands
- Wobbly legs
- Talking too fast
- Missing key information
- Knot in the stomach
- Wavering voice
- Dry mouth
- Losing direction/freezing up
- Fidgeting

You may have one or more of these symptoms. They're natural reactions to what can be a stressful situation.

Stage fright can never be entirely eliminated, but it can be managed, mostly by adequate preparation. The more you know about the subject and the more you rehearse (see the next section), the less you'll be affected by nerves. Remember the old saying, "Practice makes perfect!" Therefore, allow adequate time to prepare.

MAKE TIME TO REHEARSE

Almost everyone at some time or other has had to sit through an ill-prepared presentation: unclear objectives, no real structure, poor or inappropriate visual aids, rambling delivery, no sense of what the audience wants, running out of time, blah, blah, blah.

Before you know it you've tuned out and are surreptitiously checking your BlackBerry.

A few years ago, a board of directors instructed ten senior managers to prepare a fifteen-minute presentation outlining budget requirements for the coming financial year. Because of the number of presentations, the managers were told that the fifteen-minute deadline was mandatory. All of the managers except one stuck to this time limit and obtained what they asked for (give or take 10 percent). The manager who tried to overrun was stopped before he even reached his main point. Not surprisingly, he received significantly less than the others. He complained bitterly to his boss, saying that his presentation had taken far longer than he had anticipated. His boss asked him if he'd rehearsed and timed his presentation. Exit shame-faced manager stage left!

Therefore, ensure that you do at least one run-through . . . to your partner, a colleague, to the mirror if necessary—any "audience" will suffice. Even with good preparation, the actual delivery usually takes longer (sometimes shorter) than expected. The trial run should reveal most problems and allow you to rectify them and help reduce any natural nervousness.

Also remember to have "Plan B," an available summary slide or PowerPoint showing just the main points of your proposal in case you find yourself running short on time.

GAIN THEIR INTEREST EARLY

Who hasn't suffered through a presentation, wondering "What is this really about?" or "Why do I need to listen to this?" and of course "When is it going to be over?"

For example, a person from a Finance department spent over an hour explaining last year's results and next year's budget to a group of managers—lots of detail and "accountant-speak." After the presentation, most of the managers saw it as a waste of time. The few who had managed to "tune in" throughout the whole hour went off delighted with the prospect of having some extra cash in their budgets next year to buy desperately needed capital equipment. The others only found out later as the requests went in ("So that's what it was all about!").

If the accountant had emphasized the extra cash early on, she would have had a far more attentive audience throughout the entire presentation. But she failed to gain their interest. Many of them missed the salient point—that there was money to be spent.

So if you want people to listen, grab their attention early. The best way of doing this is to offer a benefit. Suppose the accountant had cut to the chase, and said: "I am delighted to tell you that there is $X available next year for new capital equipment, which we know you all desperately need. Before I talk about next year's budget, let's go over how everyone generated the cash this year so that we can do more of the same, hopefully with a similar effect." If you were one of those managers in the audience, would you now be listening?

BE YOURSELF

There are good public speakers, and then there are the rest of us (well, most of the rest of us, anyway). It's easy to admire an effective presenter and think: "I wish I could copy her style. Clear, confident, persuasive—I'm so jealous!" While there is nothing wrong in learning from skilled or polished presenters, difficulties occur when imitation is taken too far.

For example, during a presentation skills course, one participant gave an impression of a demented puppet, hopping around, waving his arms, and jerking his body back and forth. At first the class thought it was nerves, but later he explained that his boss had told him he was too boring and to put some life into his speech. So the man took the suggestion to heart, imitating his sales manager boss, whose style of public speaking was rather like a fire-and-brimstone preacher in the Old West. Although it may have worked for the boss, in this individual it looked downright strange and distracted from the points he was trying to make.

Although it's fine to learn from others, do not copy them. Develop your own style and, above all, be yourself! Try to capitalize on your strengths. If you're an introvert who usually talks quietly, occasionally speak louder to make a point—people will really listen. The opposite is true for boisterous personalities—if they say something more softly, it usually gets attention and has a dramatic effect (reserve such techniques for your most important points).

Analyze your weaknesses, and work out how to correct and counter them in such a way that you are comfortable. Remember, we're much more aware of our own flaws than others. Most people are so caught up in their own lives they likely won't notice quirks and mistakes unless we call attention to them.

Once the course participant relaxed and eliminated the unnatural theatrics, his presentations were far more spontaneous and interesting.

GIMME A BREAK!

Have you ever sat through a nonstop presentation for an hour or more? By the end, nature is likely calling very loudly (perhaps screaming), and rigor mortis has started in the gluteus maximus and elsewhere along the back and legs. Aside from that, you probably didn't absorb much of what was said because you (and probably everyone else there) went into "information overload." The sad part is that the presentation could have been relevant and interesting, but it was too much information (also known as TMI), over too long a time without a break.

Most people's span of concentration seems to be around twenty minutes. After that, their attention usually deteriorates rapidly.

When doing a presentation, break the information down into manageable chunks. Try to keep explanation of "blocks" of information to fifteen minutes maximum, then allow time for people to think about it and ask questions. If you have to give a long presentation, take a break at least every hour!

Say you have to inform the group about an updated computer system. The breakdown of a one-hour presentation might look like this:

- Difficulties with the present old-school system (15 min.)
- Description of the main features of the new computerized system (15 min.)
- Break (5 min.)—serve coffee?
- How people will be trained in the use of the new system (10 min.)
- Questions about the system and/or training (15 min.)

Along with organizing the information into manageable chunks, this setup allows for a variety of information, a short rest, and an opportunity to ask questions.

PICTURES ARE MEMORABLE

So many presentations seem to consist of purely verbal information or, if visual aids are used, copies of very complex charts or tables. Although PowerPoint and similar software and such Internet conferencing tools as NetMeeting or Windows Meeting Space have improved the readability of information, there's still a problem with too much verbal data. You need to pare it down to the few essential points, or better yet, use a picture.

If you are trying to make a point, which will have more impact: plowing through a detailed verbal or written explanation of the new sign or the picture shown above? Most people remember pictures better than words, provided that the picture is relevant. Showing someone a picture of a new piece of large equipment will be more memorable than simply talking about it. The same applies to easy-to-understand graphs, which were discussed in Chapter 5. For example, a simple pie chart of costs versus income not only illustrates the main point but is easily remembered by the audience. For those who want the detailed breakdown have available PowerPoint slides with the information and handouts in an easy-to-read form.

REMEMBER THE THREE Ts

A basic failing in too many presentations is that the audience has no idea what to expect. They are never told why the presentation is being given, what will be covered, or how long it will take. In short, they are left in the dark.

The presenter may know where she is going with this, but it doesn't occur to her to let the audience in on the secret. Some very brave soul might venture, "What is the point of this?" but that is extremely rare. The audience is far more likely to sit tight and hope that the purpose will eventually become clear. When it does, the audience members then have to think back over the previous ten or twenty minutes to try and remember the essential information.

When you're trying to impart information or persuade, the audience must understand the objective and the relevance of what you are saying early on. Sometimes later is too late—the presenter has already lost the audience and/or they've missed out on essential points! An easy way to avoid this is to use the "three Ts":

Tell them what you are **going** to tell them, then **actually tell** them, then **tell** them what you **have told** them.

You can apply this method to all your presentations—possibly with one or two slight additions—as follows:

1. Tell them what you are going to tell them (the objective, why you are talking to them, how you will get there, and how long they will have to listen).

2. Tell them (logical structure and keep to the point).
3. Tell them what you have told them (in summary form containing: first, essential information to remember; and second, your proposal and its chief benefits).

Don't read straight from the notes or the PowerPoint; that's an almost guarantee of losing audience interest. Some ad-libbing and even humor is helpful in preventing boredom and can spice up even the most routine information. If you're uncomfortable about doing this, try practicing in front of the mirror or with a trusted colleague/family member a few times. The more familiar you are with the material, the less likely you'll rely on your notes, and the more natural and spontaneous your presentation will sound. (See "Make Time to Rehearse" on page 130 for additional suggestions.)

COVER THE SNAGS AS WELL AS THE BENEFITS

We all have pride of authorship in our ideas. We thought up the proposal, there are significant benefits to be gained from adopting it, and we are going to sell it for all it's worth! Nothing wrong with that, you might think—you have to believe in something to sell it well. However, some people become almost evangelical about their proposal and lose sight of reality, viewing their idea with rose-tinted glasses.

In their enthusiasm, they only state the benefits and never admit to any snags. This behavior stems from a belief that mentioning any problems will diminish their case. Ignoring potential difficulties or inefficiencies may have worked in the past, but given the bottom-line atmosphere of corporate America, such a rose-tinted approach will be looked upon with skepticism at best. How would you react to two proposals, the first of which only outlined the benefits, and the second, which discussed both benefits and the snags?

You can cover both good and bad aspects of the proposal and still be enthusiastic. You should be able to prove that potential problems are outweighed by the benefits—otherwise why present the proposal at all? This gives the person you're pitching to proof that you have considered both sides of the matter. Be sure to show how the snags can either be eliminated or reduced.

ANTICIPATE TOUGH QUESTIONS

Have you ever seen an otherwise excellent presentation disintegrate during the question stage at the end? Not much fun when that happens.

Some presenters seem to adopt the "ostrich" principle. They bury their heads in the sand and ignore potentially tough questions in the hope that they will not arise. This is dangerous thinking indeed. Pretending tough questions don't exist is like ignoring an elephant in your living room—both loom large and indisputable. In fact, *not* addressing these issues might generate criticism. When you have your back to the wall, there are those who will try to move in for the kill and discredit you and your idea.

At the preparation stage of a proposal, consider the very worst questions that might be asked and decide whether:

1. They should be raised and answered by you during the presentation; or
2. They should be left to the audience to ask at the end.

In the first case, build the questions and your answers into the content of the presentation. In the second case, decide broadly what your answers will be if these questions come up.

If you are unsure as to what questions may arise, ask someone who has some knowledge in this or a similar field and encourage him to generate the worst-case scenario he can think of. Often, asking your own manager might help—she has probably been in a similar situation. As mentioned in Chapter 8, if a question arises to which you do not know the answer, say so! Tell the questioner you'll get back to her with the information, and make sure that you do so within the necessary time frame.

REMEMBER TO ASK FOR APPROVAL

The objective is to gain acceptance for a proposal, but sometimes you can inadvertently undermine yourself. Say the proposal is clear, the advantages and benefits well stated, the risks minor and easily handled, and you finish with a good summary of key points and efficiently answer questions that arise. So far, so good. However, you neglect to ask for approval for your proposal. Instead, because you leave at the end of the presentation, you have little or no additional opportunity to influence the outcome!

Even the most confident presenters may hesitate when asking, "Now that you have heard the idea, can I go ahead with it?" Why does this reticence occur? It is due to a fear of rejection. Nobody likes to hear "No." But is that any reason for not asking? Being told "No" is better than not knowing at all.

So at the end of your presentation, remember to ask for approval. This can be easily done by using a PowerPoint or other slide with the heading "Next Steps" or something similar. Or you can ask point-blank, "I have outlined why I think we should do A, B, and C. Can I go ahead?" Consider the possible responses:

- "No." This is the answer everyone fears. You can ask, "Why?" and attempt to handle the objection then and there. Taking the worst case, however, if the reason for "No" is one you can't counter, at least you have learned something for next time.
- "I like the idea but . . ." Clarify the "but . . ." and see if you can find a way of handling it.
- "Yes," in which case you have achieved what you wanted and can proceed with the proposal.

- "Give me a couple of days to think about it." If the proposal has far-reaching implications, this is quite reasonable. Set a date for the next meeting, at which you'll get your answer.

It is often said that we learn more from our failures than successes. If this is true, then you'll want to get as much mileage as you can from the experience, even if the outcome isn't what you'd hoped for.

TAKE-AWAY POINTS

- The best way to combat nerves is to be prepared. A trial run or rehearsal will help you anticipate how long the presentation will take and will allow you to be familiar and comfortable with it.
- At the beginning of your presentation, hook the audience with a vital point of interest. Always offer them a benefit that will keep them listening.
- Although it's fine to study the example of polished presenters, be yourself. Otherwise you may come off as unnatural or even worse, strange.
- Organize the presentation into bite-sized chunks of information and allow for breaks and questions.
- Use pictures and other illustrations to illustrate your point. A picture is indeed worth a thousand words.
- Remember the three "Ts"—tell people what you're going to say, then actually tell them, and then tell them what you've told them.
- Cover the snags as well as the benefits as someone will likely ask the inevitable tough questions. By ignoring the latter you may be setting yourself up for even worse criticism.
- After the presentation is over, ask for approval. The worst that can happen is "No" and you can learn from that if you ask "Why?"

CHAPTER 11

Mastering the Meeting

CHAPTER OBJECTIVES

To understand how to decide if a meeting is the best means of achieving the objective

To learn to make meetings results-oriented

To discover the main principles of running effective meetings

To see how conferences, conventions, and retreats can also be a source of new ideas

INTRODUCTION

Ask people how they feel about meetings and in most cases there is a negative reaction, usually because people usually feel that meetings accomplish very little.

Someone once defined a committee as a group of the unwilling, picked from the unfit, to do the unnecessary. Unfortunately, some meetings can seem just like that, but they don't have to be. By using a few fairly simple guidelines, meetings can be productive and—dare we say it—(almost) fun.

ORGANIZING MEETINGS AND OBTAINING RESULTS

Meetings are an exchange of ideas, information, or opinions by a group of people who play an active role to achieve specific results. This is in contrast to conferences (discussed in "Conferences, Conventions, and Retreats" on page 153) in which most of the audience is in passive mode, listening to a series of speakers. Unlike most meetings, which only have a few people, conferences can have dozens if not hundreds of participants.

The most frequent criticism of meetings is that "they don't achieve much." People are quite prepared to put effort into a meeting if they can see a result. But it is extremely frustrating to do your homework, then find that there is no real outcome. "We only talked. Nothing was decided!" If this happens, it's not too surprising that the reaction to the next invitation is: "Not another meeting—what a waste of time!"

ARE MEETINGS NECESSARY?

Some managers automatically seem to call meetings if there is anything to discuss, without ever appearing to consider whether a meeting is the best way to communicate.

Have you ever been in a meeting where a significant portion of it was a conversation between the chairperson and one or two other participants? Quite frequently the others are wondering why they have to sit there for twenty minutes listening to something that is irrelevant (to them) and that could have been handled via e-mail, a telephone call, or a smaller meeting.

Other people call a meeting to impart information that could easily be e-mailed or otherwise distributed in written form. A good example of this would the announcement of a revised but straightforward procedure. If no discussion or clarification of the procedure is necessary, why call a meeting?

Decide what your objectives are, and determine the best method of achieving each one. You should consider the following options *before* calling a meeting:

- Send out written information via e-mail or other distribution with the option to ask questions if necessary
- Phone call
- One-on-one discussion
- Subgroup meeting, with specific objectives
- Full group meeting, again with specific objectives

Often a full group meeting is the most inefficient way of communicating, but it is the method some people always seem to use!

FOCUS ON RESULTS, RATHER THAN ON SUBJECTS

An agenda for a meeting is intended not only as a checklist for the chairperson, but also to help participants prepare. Most agendas seem to be based on subjects rather than on objectives, so the content may read as follows:

- Minutes of the last meeting
- Progress on computer project
- Lunchtime phone cover
- Improving communications
- Any other business

This will remind the chairperson of the subjects to be covered and in what order, but if you were to receive that agenda as a participant, could you adequately prepare for the meeting? Unless you knew the background behind each of the headings, probably not. Participants usually also want a meeting to achieve results, but with this type of agenda they can only guess at the underlying intention. When setting an agenda, make sure to include results-oriented objectives. For example, based on the original agenda above:

- Confirm that actions agreed on at the last meeting are taken.
- Decide actions, individual responsibilities, and deadlines for phase three of the computer project.
- Set up and agree on a workable schedule for lunchtime phone cover in our department.
- Decide how to find out how our customers (internal and external) feel about the service we provide and discuss who should take care of which problem area defined by customers.

This agenda may lengthen the meeting, but the outcomes will be worth it, and in the long term may result in fewer meetings.

KEEPING MEETINGS SHORT AND TO THE POINT

Do you attend or run meetings that contain "Any other business" (AOB) on the agenda? AOB supposedly allows time to cover any additional issues not listed on the agenda; typically the rubbish that nobody can find a slot for. Frequently the same old subjects come up every time: for instance, Harry moaning about his wobbly chair (for the ninth time). Even when sensible issues are mentioned, the rest of the group has had no notice and therefore often lacks the necessary information to contribute to the discussion. The next ten minutes is spent deciding that nothing can be decided yet. Not very productive!

If you are the chairperson, encourage people to give you their objectives before the agenda is finalized. Tell them that, as of the next meeting, AOB will no longer exist. They must notify you of these issues and provide you with an estimate of the time they think it will take to discuss the topic. If a genuine "crisis" occurs immediately prior to the meeting, either agree to extend the meeting time or drop a less important item.

If you are a participant, you might be able to suggest the idea of removing AOB privately to the chairperson.

START YOUR MEETINGS ON TIME

First impressions count! People learn very quickly whether or not your meetings start on time and usually act accordingly. First one person comes in ten minutes late, next time three people will be fifteen minutes late, and it goes downhill after that.

Often the chairperson has to delay discussion of an item (because the latecomer's input is needed) or call an unnecessary coffee break (they have only just finished the scheduled break) in order to locate the latecomer. When the latecomer does eventually arrive, what does the chairperson do? Summarizes! Consequently, the latecomer learns that no matter when he shows up, he will be brought up to date—which hardly encourages prompt future attendance.

What about the people who were organized enough to be present for the start of the meeting? They are on your side, trying to help you by being there on time. Yet it is their time that is being wasted.

There are a several ways to handle this:

- Ask yourself whether the latecomer's tardiness is justifiable. If it's a superior or someone important to the organization or goals of the meeting, you may want to wait a little longer to start and/or bring them up to speed when they arrive. Not to do so shows a lack of respect and will likely run counter to the goals of your team and the meeting.
- If the person is a peer and/or someone who's on an equal footing with the rest of the attendees and their tardiness is becoming a habit, try ignoring them (apart from "Hello, Ken . . . now what were you saying, Marion?") for about five minutes—then summarize. The short period of being ignored is uncomfortable for the latecomer (and he doesn't know that it will only be five minutes). You owe it to the people who took the trouble to be there promptly to prevent the latecomer's arrival from disrupting the meeting. It shows consideration for them, and discourages those who meander in at their own convenience.

Another exception is if the meeting is being held "virtually" via NetMeeting, Windows Meeting Space, or some other software. A few minutes' leeway is needed, as everyone may not have synchronized clocks, and participants are usually in different locations. Don't forget to coordinate time zones, as in "the meeting will be held at 10 A.M. EST."

After "starting time" on the agenda, write "sharp please" and ensure that you actually start your meeting at that time. People will quickly learn that you mean it: "Better go. Karen's meetings always begin promptly."

SET A FINISH TIME

Do the meetings you attend have a declared finish time? Many meetings lack a set finish time, so you have to try to figure out how long it will take and organize your day around that. Following are some reasons why finish times are *not* set:

- No one thought of doing it.
- The chairperson has no idea how long the meeting will take or had not given much thought to it.
- The chairperson does not want to limit discussion.

How often have you sat in a meeting and wondered: "How much longer is this going to take? They are talking it to death!"

Declaring a specific finish time seems to focus the mind, because you have to accomplish a discussion of X item in Y number of minutes. Like giving yourself a deadline to do something, or putting it on a "To do" list, setting time limits encourages organization and productivity.

However, be realistic when establishing a finish time. In some ways, it's more of an art than a science, requiring a "guesstimate" of how long each objective on the agenda is going to take. At first, until you get a "sense" of it, allow an extra fifteen to thirty minutes to cover all items you're unsure of. The more you work with this type of agenda-setting, the more skilled you'll become. It's also helpful to ask an experienced chairperson to give you some guidelines and suggestions.

If the meeting takes longer than an hour, put time limits for each subject on the agenda to keep things moving and ensure content is covered. Also for longer meetings set forth certain rules of conduct limiting, for example, cell phone use, and how long an individual can speak on a particular topic, to avoid "dominators" (grown-up versions of kids who always raise their hands in class).

Also, try to stay away from setting meetings that will last for more than an hour. People's concentration starts to wander after this length of time, if not before. If you do have to hold a long meeting, build in breaks (also discussed in the previous chapter) or consider holding shorter sub-meetings on certain topics.

CURTAIL TOPIC DRIFT IN BOTH MINUTES AND DISCUSSION

Do the minutes of a meeting you receive a week later sometimes bear little resemblance to what actually transpired?

What typically happens is that the chairperson, who is usually also responsible for note-taking, scribbles furiously while trying to control the meeting. First, it is hard to perform both roles (chairperson and "secretary") simultaneously—one or the other usually suffers. To take a cynical view, some chairpersons, if unsure, write down what they wanted to hear anyway. Second, you and the other attendees cannot see what is being jotted down, so you don't know whether the notes match or even relate to what was just said. These factors set the stage for errors.

When chairing a meeting, consider asking someone to act as an assistant. They can take notes in several ways: low-tech, by using a flip chart; on a laptop/computer that hooks onto a projector screen; or via a wipe-off bulletin board or electronic "white board" such as on NetMeeting. Regardless of how it's done, the information will be visible to everyone. If a mistake occurs, it will be easily spotted and corrected.

You can then issue the contents of the flip chart/computer printout/board as "minutes." Often, most people only want to know what was decided, what has to be done, by whom, and by when. Try asking those at the meeting what they want the minutes to contain. Most will say "Keep it simple!"

Another dilemma occurs when a manager is chairing a meeting and also has to be a leading contributor to one or more agenda items. As a contributor, the need is to input or discuss information, whereas, as chairperson, the role is to control the input and ensure that it is relevant to the objective(s).

This results in a potential conflict of interest, making it easy to talk too much on the topic or try to manipulate events in your favor. Furthermore, most people who attend meetings are reluctant to try and call the chairperson to order (especially if that person is their boss as well).

Consider using a "stand-in" to chair the portion of the meeting where you need to act as a leading contributor. It is an excellent development opportunity for someone who is working toward a management position. Also:

1. Discuss the objective(s) with your stand-in before the meeting to ensure she understands what you are trying to achieve.
2. When handing over the chair during the meeting, explain that the stand-in will control the next item(s), and that includes your input.

If you have to be a prominent contributor throughout most of the meeting, you might want to let your stand-in chair the entire meeting

HANDLING UNEXPECTED SITUATIONS

A common question, especially among beginning managers, is: "How do I, as chairperson, handle the situation where my boss (or someone else senior) turns up and takes over the meeting? Not only is it annoying but it makes me look unnecessary!" This difficulty does not (usually) arise from rudeness but from two other factors:

1. Senior people are used to chairing meetings and there-fore tend to fall naturally into the role without meaning to disrupt.
2. Those attending the meeting tend to address questions and comments to the most senior person present rather than to the chairperson, especially if the senior person arrives unexpectedly.

If you fear that this situation might (or already has) occurred, try discussing it privately with the senior person involved. Although you can't change what happened in past meetings, you can prevent future difficulties. You might try the following approach:

- Constructively explain how you felt and the difficulties it caused (or what you feel could potentially happen).
- Outline your objectives for the next meeting, and then find out what the senior person expects from the meeting.
- Ask the senior person to suggest how best to conduct the meeting to meet both your needs and theirs. Most senior people understand and are helpful. You should then be able to decide your respective roles and agree on an appropriate plan for the meeting.

Additionally, you might try asking other team members for opinions on the content during the meeting to avoid allowing the boss to dominate. This is a good tactic when dealing with anyone who tends to dominate meetings.

ENSURE THAT PARTICIPANTS UNDERSTAND THEIR ROLE

Have you ever attended a meeting where you thought the objective was to make a decision, only to find that the decision was to be made by someone else and you were simply being consulted?

For example, at a meeting with an agenda item of new software, the group thought they were going to be asked to discuss requirements and decide what new software would be of benefit to the department. Before the meeting they talked about possible useful additions. As the meeting progressed, however, it became clear that the manager only wanted to consult them about their ideas so that she could decide on the final list of software, also taking into account the needs of a second section reporting to her. The group saw their role as "decision-making," but the manager saw their role as "providing information." This point was not clarified until thirty minutes into the agenda item.

As mentioned before, clear objectives are vital. However, even some seemingly obvious results-oriented objectives may not make the role of the *participants* clear.

As part of the introduction to each objective on the agenda, the chairperson should ensure that the role of the participants is made clear. The following questions might help:

- Are they being consulted for their views prior to a decision being made elsewhere?
- Are they making the decision or producing a recommendation?
- Are they discussing the implementation of a decision made elsewhere?

GET A COMMITMENT TO ACT

Consider the following example. The meeting went well, and everyone seemed comfortable with the outcome and action plan. At the next meeting, progress was discussed, and Fred suddenly commented: "Well, I didn't actually agree to do that, you know. You just assumed that I would." To which you reply, "But I'm sure you agreed to it last time."

Most people try their best to take the necessary action by the given deadline. There are some, however, who seem to make a career out of avoiding any responsibility. They succeed because no one says specifically: "Fred, will you take responsibility for . . . ?" Sometimes we assume agreement. If the person says nothing, it is assumed that he or she has accepted the consensus.

So insist upon a "public" agreement by each person to take the relevant action by a specific date. A simple "yes" on their part in front of the group will suffice. Any misunderstanding will then be avoided at that point. This is made easier if you are using a visual aid with the "what, who, and by when" format. The action plan should be clear to everyone. Add a column headed "Agreed" to the right of the "What," "Who" and "By when" columns on the visual.

Having produced the action plan, ask every person involved if they agree to the actions listed for them, and, on agreement, tick the action item. You may only be doing this in fact for one person (who always tries to wriggle out of responsibility), but it is important to apply it to all. You can easily explain it as helping you to check that you (or the assistant) have recorded all points accurately.

CONFERENCES, CONVENTIONS, AND RETREATS

A more exciting (and expensive!) alternative to meetings and routine forms of information exchange is to have you and your team attend a conference, convention, or retreat. Each has a role to play in learning and maintaining skills needed by your organization.

A *conference* is a prearranged meeting for consultation or interchange of information or discussion (especially one with a formal agenda). A *convention* is a large formal assembly of those with like interests, such as a convention of pipefitters or dentists. A *retreat* offers a place of privacy and peace, for prayer, study, or meditation. For purposes here, conferences and conventions are interchangeable. Advantages include a chance to network and exchange new ideas as well as expand opportunities for your business. Conferences usually also offer the latest cutting edge information and technology in the field, allowing you to stay abreast and be current. Although they may not pay out initially, in the long run they generally add to your overall knowledge and create new ideas. Many conferences are energizing and inspiring, as you get to know others in your field with the same interests and can consult with them and get solutions or feedback when problems or other issues arise.

In contrast, retreats generally involve a much smaller number of people, usually within the same company or organization. Goals of a retreat are a bit loftier: strategic planning, "vision" and priority setting, role clarification, and decision-making.

Adventure Associates Teambuilding,[19] a company that focuses on retreats and team building for *Fortune* 500 and other companies, makes the following recommendations when considering a retreat:

1. Invite the right people . . . don't use retreats as rewards if it excludes key team members.
2. Have clear objectives for the retreat and commit them to a highly focused agenda.
3. Be a good time manager during the retreat . . . don't let conversations go on tangents . . . request that small groups take topics offline if they don't impact the entire team.
4. Assign homework before the workshop to make the most of your time together.
5. Keep an action list on hand to track commitments, responsible parties, and deadlines.
6. Build a postretreat follow-up into the process . . . future improvements depend on this.
7. Use a neutral retreat facilitator so that the team members are free to focus on the content of the retreat rather than just the logistics.

(Source: Adventure Associates, Inc., *www.adventureassoc.com*)

By their very nature, meetings and other "routine" aspects of the everyday workplace can be tedious and at worst, annoying. Conferences/conventions and retreats offer a great way to boost morale and encourage new ideas, as well as to renew commitment to the company or organization.

TAKE-AWAY POINTS

• Before setting up or organizing a meeting, ask yourself: Is a meeting the best way?

- The agenda should show results-oriented objectives rather than subjects.
- Eliminate "Any other business" from agendas.
- Start your meetings on time and set a finish time. Be firm about these, and nicely let latecomers know that their behavior is unacceptable.
- Consider using an assistant and visual aids for clarity.
- Consider using a "stand-in" chair when you need to become involved in the content.
- Prehandle potential difficulties when more senior people attend your meeting.
- Ensure that participants understand their role.
- By the end of the meeting, get a definite commitment to act from team members.
- Consider sending your team—and/or going yourself—to a conference, convention, or retreat. You'll likely come back with new ideas and renewed enthusiasm.

CHAPTER 12

Improving Performance

CHAPTER OBJECTIVES

To learn how to work with employees to improve their performance

To understand why it's important to be able to communicate clearly and fairly with team members regarding performance and other issues

To comprehend how to handle sensitive issues, such as dealing with personal problems and employee discipline

INTRODUCTION

In Chapter 8, we discussed coaching and how, in many ways, it has replaced counseling in the workplace. Many principles of coaching are used to help employees who fall short of requirements to improve their performance. However, managers should work with all team members in this area, even those who operate at a high level. Often these individuals are eager to find new and better ways of doing things and, if properly motivated, can set the stage for the entire team's improved performance. Also to be considered are those at a "normal" level of performance; that is, they are neither high- or underachievers.

COACHING AND IMPROVING PERFORMANCE

Chapter 8 discussed coaching as it relates to building teams; many of these principles can also be applied to improving employee performance. In many ways it's a matter of semantics. Rather than telling employees you're "counseling" them, use the word *coaching*, which has a more positive connotation. Regardless of the terminology, as a manager you're helping the individual explore, identify, and own their performance strengths and weaknesses and enabling them to find ways to improve.

Management involves getting results; that's how most managers are measured. Getting results means helping all team members work at their maximum performance level. Therefore coaching and communicating with team members on how they can improve their performance will help you achieve your goals.

MAKE SURE WORKERS OWN THEIR RESPONSIBILITIES

The best way to help someone understand that there is a weakness (and also a strength) without actually telling him is to encourage ownership; that is, by reaching a point where the individual acknowledges his strength or weakness.

For example, a section leader on your team staunchly refuses to delegate any of his workload. As a direct result, he is doing vast amounts of the more difficult routine work but not the planning and distribution so vital to his role. You call him in to discuss the problem and he insists that he can do it quicker and better than anyone else. You tell him to delegate more, and you clearly explain how to start. Off he goes, and what happens? Nothing! Because he did not believe he was doing anything wrong in the first place. He was doing his very best to produce the work from a busy section. In short, he did not own the problem you had identified.

Telling someone that there is a problem does not mean he believes you. When you were a youngster and your mom or dad reprimanded you for coming home late from a party, did you believe then that you had done anything wrong? "They are being unreasonable." "They don't understand." "They are old," would all have been fairly typical reactions.

Ownership is best achieved via effective questioning. For example:

- What do you see as your strengths/areas for improvement?
- What are the benefits/likely consequences of that strength/ weakness?

"But what if they still don't accept it?" you may wonder. Then rather than tell them, use factual evidence and present it in a logical, nonconfrontational way. "Andrea, you say you get on well with everyone, but this morning you were having a very heated argument with Mark. You also had one with Karen on Monday."

REVIEW PERFORMANCE OBJECTIVELY—STRENGTHS ARE JUST AS IMPORTANT AS WEAKNESSES

Make sure that the evaluation discussion is balanced. Every team member has strengths and weaknesses. For example, consider how the following two managers deal with performance situations:

- **Mr. Teddy Bear:** A very pleasant and understanding manager. Everything is rosy, all is going well, and the only form of "coaching" he gives you is to tell you what a super job you are doing and how important you are to the organization. As far as he is concerned you never ever do anything wrong and, if a problem does occur, he appreciates that it is all due to someone else, or the computer system, and so on.
- **Ms. Rhino:** Often bad-tempered or grumpy, she charges head-on at the least provocation! When she coaches you, you wonder if you ever do anything right in her view. She seems to worry too much about minor shortfalls (for example, spelling mistakes in a report), yet gives you no credit for getting the important things right (for example, doubling sales).

If you have had the misfortune to work for either character, you will know exactly how it feels! Most people want (and expect) feedback from their manager and they hope it will be objective and balanced—tell it as it really is and focus on the important things.

So in evaluating performance or critiquing team members ensure that you cover both sides of the equation, including:

- Strengths, and how they can be used even more
- Areas for improvement, and how to achieve the improvement

ASK OPEN-ENDED QUESTIONS

Following is a typical conversation between a well-meaning manager and a reticent team member:

Manager: "Are things OK at home?"
Team member: "Fine!"
Manager: "Any problems with workload?"
Team member: "No."
Manager: "Is the computer working properly?"
Team member: "Yes, it's fine." And so on.

Does this remind you of trying to get information from an adolescent? If you've ever attempted to do so, you quickly learn that straightforward questions, or ones that require "yes" or "no" answers, usually end up hitting the wall, resulting in little or no information. A more effective tactic is required, one that involves asking open-ended or indirect questions.

Open-ended questions usually start with "what, where, when, who, how, or why" and therefore collect useful information. For example:

- "What effect is the new computer system having?"
- "Why do you think that is happening?"
- "How do you think we could solve that?"

They can be probing and relate to specifics. For example: "Why do you think a training course is the answer?"

Indirect questions are a little more subtle. Rather than approaching the subject head-on, use a question to elicit a sympathetic response, which will sometimes get the more reticent to open up. For example, instead of saying, "What do you think of the Vista operating system?" which the employee might construe as wanting only positive feedback, you can say, "I'm having all kinds of trouble with the Vista operating system. What's your experience?"

OFFER OPTIONS RATHER THAN ADVICE

Be careful in using the word *advice* when talking to your employees or communicating the impression that you are about to give them advice. Ask yourself what could happen:

- If it is good advice on a simple issue, the team member is grateful for the help and the suggested action(s) works.
- If it is good advice, and the team member does not agree or believe in it, it might fail because they have no or little commitment to it.
- If it is inappropriate for that person/situation but the manager/team member doesn't realize this, then the advice is likely to go wrong.

People generally give advice because they are trying to help. The advice is often quite valid if it relates to something that the team member could not be expected to know (for example, who to see in order to learn more about the invoicing system).

However, when the situation is more complex, it is better—and safer—to offer options, and encourage the team member to do the choosing. For example: "We have agreed that some basic computer training would help you. The options are an external course within a month, an internal course in four months, or spend time now with Fred, who knows our system well. Which works best for you?"

RESPECT PAUSES

In a difficult situation, most people are uncomfortable with pauses. When we are out of our comfort zone a pause seems to make things even more awkward.

Next time you are at home, say, with friends you have known for a long time, try this exercise. Sitting in the living room with a cup of coffee after dinner, chatting about nothing in particular, watch for pauses in the conversation. There will probably be quite long pauses, yet nobody bothers with or possibly even notices them. The relationships are strong enough for the pauses not to worry anyone present. People aren't thinking, "I must say something because the conversation has dried up."

Coaching is not always a comfortable process (even when praising good performance), so the manager is concerned about pauses and often tries to fill the gap. For example: "Well, Marion, how do you think we could tackle that? . . . (five-second pause) . . . I think perhaps we should revise the system." This doesn't give Marion a chance to reply.

Although it may feel uncomfortable, accept that pauses are necessary, and do not try to fill the silence. Often the questions asked during these sessions are tough, which means that people need thinking time. Try to resist the natural temptation to fill the silence. Ask the question, then have a sip of coffee if it helps. Remember that you need their answer, not yours.

LOOK AT BEHAVIOR, NOT PERSONALITY

Some managers have a tendency to describe difficulties in "personality" terms:

- "Andrea has an attitude problem."
- "Mark is downright obstructive."
- "Damion lacks any sort of spark."
- "Camilla is far too aggressive."

Try telling someone they are aggressive or obstructive. People do not take kindly to that sort of observation. A common response is: "What do you mean, I'm obstructive?"

Personality traits are hard to change (ask any psychiatrist). If the person has a particular trait, odds are you will be unable to alter it. However, one aspect can be changed—*behavior*—so focus the discussion on that.

Consider how the difficulty manifests itself. For example, which of his actions tell you that Mark is obstructive? The answer might be: "Mark resists every change, can never see any good in any suggestions, and always starts by saying he won't do it."

Because you have defined specific behaviors, you can address them with Mark so he has a clear view of what he's doing wrong. Rather than the abstract trait of "obstructive," you can discuss particular instances far more easily. Mark may not change how he feels inside, but he can take actions to stop behaving obstructively.

Also, when giving feedback on behavior, choose your words carefully. Using phrases such as "From my viewpoint" or "I have observed" reduces the chance that the individual will become defensive as well as increasing the likelihood that she or he will act upon the feedback.

MATCH SOLUTIONS WITH PROBLEMS

A quick and easy way to deal with performance issues is to "put the employee in a course" with the assumption that that will fix everything. Say, for example, Jane is shy and soft-spoken and has a hard time standing up for herself. As someone who works in the admissions office in a busy hospital, she needs to be more assertive. Rather than sitting down with her and discussing ways she can improve, her supervisor sends her to a class on assertiveness, hoping she will "get the hint."

Maybe she will, but the manager is shirking her responsibility and avoiding the problem. Rather than just assigning team members to a training course, assess their needs objectively and explain why they are being sent to the course and what you hope they'll get from it.

Consider which of the following approaches might best meet the team member's need. More than one approach might be required.

- Short training course (internal or external)
- Longer-term learning
- Reading company-produced information
- Coaching by manager
- Coaching by colleague/trainer
- "Shadowing" (observing the manager)
- Anything else you, as a manager or your team member, might think works

Making sure the approach fits the situation being addressed will go a long way toward solving the problem and providing the team member with insight, understanding, and ideas for solutions.

AVOID PERSONAL PROBLEMS AND PSYCHOANALYSIS

Most managers try to understand the people on their team, but some indulge in amateur psychology. This can be dangerous because psychologists (and other mental health professionals) train for years in their attempt to comprehend the nuances of human behavior. Attempting to "get into someone's head" to resolve their mental problems is akin to trying to fix a gas leak yourself. Both can easily result in an explosion.

Still, some managers draw deep, meaningful inferences about what a team member is thinking, then, even worse, act on those conclusions. When asked if they in fact talked to the individual concerned, they reply: "No need to. I know what makes them tick!" That is very questionable! Even professional psychologists are unlikely to ever claim that. People are very complex, and fully understanding them and their motives is a difficult (if not impossible) undertaking.

When dealing with any problem, keep it simple. Ask people how they feel and what they believe would be the best actions and why. Then build on their responses, if possible. But be careful not to impose your possibly incorrect assumptions on them.

Avoid Trying to Solve Problems from Outside Work

Managers need to tread carefully whenever team members' personal lives are involved. Unlike a priest or a lawyer, you are in no way bound by confessional privilege. So if the team member tells you something that's against the law or company policy (such as a code of conduct violation) you are obligated to report or otherwise act on it. Employees need to be aware of this as well.

For example, say Jim's productivity has dropped 30 percent. You call Jim into your office to discuss the matter and discover that the cause of the problem is his failure to adequately understand a new procedure. With work-related issues of this kind, the solution is fairly straightforward. You arrange for Jim to have some extra training and soon he's back up to speed. With work-related situations, you are well within your authority to act.

However, suppose the cause of this performance drop turns out to be that his partner of many years left him, so he's been unable to concentrate. Then all the rules change. As a manager you have no direct authority over his personal life. Nor can you "solve" the problem, as much as you may sympathize with his plight.

Remember that your team member has already paid you a significant compliment by confiding in you at all. Having found out that the cause lies outside work, discuss with him what role he wishes you to play, and decide if that role is acceptable to you. For example, he may want or need you to act simply as a trusted and understanding listener. It is up to you to determine whether or not that is appropriate, given the constraints of your managerial position and company policy. You cannot, and should not, attempt to solve his problem—in reality, only he can do that. As mentioned in "Offer Options Rather Than Advice" on page 163, avoid giving advice.

Ask him to outline what he thinks his options are. If he appears to be stuck, suggest some possible alternatives or encourage him to get outside help. After that, set a date to talk with him again.

If an outside situation affects the team members' work (which it probably has; hence the conversation with you, the manager), find out what they think might ease the burden. Options that are within your duties as a manager include offering a more flexible schedule or a temporary shift in responsibilities (within the constraints of company policy and applicable union agreements). You can also suggest places where the employee might get help or additional resources—like for instance, finding out if his health plan covers counseling or checking on the availability of company-paid Employee Assistance Plans and/or legal consultations.

MEET WITH TEAM MEMBERS REGULARLY

What is the first thought most people have when the boss calls them into the office? It's usually something like, "Uh-oh! What have I done this time?" Unfortunately, most people react this way because that's what previous experience has taught them.

Some managers still only pull their employees aside for a talk when performance is poor. These managers often see this approach as the most effective use of their time. Consequently, people come to associate such discussions with being called on the carpet.

Often, therefore, when the team member arrives at your office, she likely has decided the discussion will be something negative. Such mind-sets are difficult to overcome. The employee is on the defensive and expecting censure—not at all the right atmosphere for coaching and improving performance!

The most effective way to counter this is to meet every member of your team regularly—say, once a month, for an hour with each individual—to discuss performance. Performance discussions and/or coaching then become the norm, and the negative perception disappears. Although it takes more time, the results will be worth it, both in communication and improved efficiency of operations.

EMPLOYEE DISCIPLINE—A CALL TO IMPROVEMENT

In a perfect world, every employee would enjoy her job and do everything she was supposed to. But in reality, there are team members who, for some reason or another, repeatedly make the same (or different) mistakes, have poor attitudes, or exhibit behaviors that are unacceptable in the workplace. You, as a manager, must deal with these individuals promptly, fairly, and firmly. Otherwise, like the proverbial bad apple, their actions will affect and eventually undermine the entire team. Generally speaking, there are two reasons for employee discipline:[20]

1. Performance problems. Team members are not meeting their goals, whether it's making a certain quota of sales or producing X amount of widgets. Generally these types of issues are easily quantifiable and documented.
2. Misconduct. This involves behavior unacceptable to both you as a manager and the organization. For example, Jane is calling in sick twice a week, or acting in an inappropriate manner, such as making racial remarks or harassing other employees. Sometimes it may be more difficult to document occurrences, so make sure to keep detailed records whenever possible.

Discipline should be handled in a progressive manner. When the problem first manifests itself, it's time for an informal chat. Often that does the trick, but if repeated gentle reminders fail to have any effect, you must move on to the next level, which will be discussed further in Chapter 13. Some misconduct may be governed by more stringent disciplinary action as dictated by company policy. Many companies have zero-tolerance policies regarding sexual harassment and violence in the workplace. As a manager you are responsible for knowing your company's procedures for investigation and disciplinary action.

Whenever possible, put a positive spin on discipline, couching it as a "call to improvement" rather than a punitive action. Also always make sure to follow company policy *to the letter* regarding discipline. Unfortunately, sometimes disciplinary situations end up in court, so you need to make sure all your actions are fully and correctly documented.

WHEN TO BRING IN OUTSIDE SPECIALISTS

When faced with a chronic problem, many managers find it extremely hard to know where to draw the line: "Where should I stop and let people with more experience/knowledge take over?"

Some people feel that, as the managers, they should be able to cope with or help in all matters affecting their team members. In truth, they are being very unfair both to themselves and their employees. Suppose, for instance, a manager suspects that a team member is drinking too much and this has started to affect his work. The manager talks to the individual, and he admits the problem but says he can't stop even though he has tried. Now what? The manager has neither the relevant expertise nor professional training to handle the situation and in fact may do more harm than good.

In such cases, prevention is the best solution. Familiarize yourself with the company's policy/procedure regarding alcohol, drug abuse, and any other issues that might require specialist help. Ask your personnel people specifically what action should be taken regarding these situations, and follow their advice. Being prepared to face such problems before they occur is far superior to second-guessing and possibly causing even more damage.

TAKE-AWAY POINTS

• Instill a sense of ownership by helping team members recognize their own strengths and weaknesses.

- Be balanced in performance reviews, discussing both good and bad points, and ask open-ended questions to obtain specific feedback.
- Rather than giving advice, suggest options from which the team member can choose.
- Although they may feel uncomfortable, especially in a difficult situation, allow for pauses in the conversation. It gives the other person time to think and provide needed answers.
- Look at and try to address the person's behavioral issues rather than personality traits. Rather than saying they are "rude," find specific actions for them to correct ("You hung up on John without saying good-bye.").
- Avoid personal problems and psychoanalysis. Know where to draw the line and when to get outside help or consultants.
- Meeting with team members on a regular basis dispels the stigma and fear of being called into the boss's office.
- Make sure to follow company procedures in disciplining employees. Such issues should be dealt with promptly, fairly, and firmly.
- Familiarize yourself with company policy regarding employee discipline, substance abuse, and other violations. That way, you will be prepared in advance and avoid serious mistakes.

CHAPTER 13

You're Hired! You're Fired!

CHAPTER OBJECTIVES

To help managers define job requirements and identify appropriate candidates when hiring

To provide guidance as to when to use "gut feelings" and when to focus on more logical reasons in hiring

To offer guidelines regarding handling performance problems, misconduct, and firing

INTRODUCTION

Hiring and firing are two of the toughest issues managers have to face. This chapter will cover the basics; as a manager, you'll need to continually add to your store of knowledge on these subjects as you develop and motivate your team.

This chapter will also help you differentiate between what you feel is right and what may actually be best for your management objectives. Many hiring decisions are made on the gut level, which can be both a good and a bad thing.

Hiring decisions are crucial and involve more than liking the individual or being charmed by the applicant. Often the seemingly less dynamic person has more to offer, especially in terms of loyalty and hard work.

Firing can be a painful and onerous task. But if handled properly, it will benefit both you and your organization in the long run, as you replace the fired employee with someone who is better suited to the team and its goals.

DEFINE THE JOB AND THE QUALIFICATIONS

When hiring, the first question managers need to ask is whether the position is new or an existing one. If it's new, you can start from scratch and come up with tasks and responsibilities that seem to best suit the job. However, make sure that what you are looking for is realistic. For example, you can't expect a computer troubleshooter to be able to do sales or public relations. If it's an existing position, you'll have a basis to work from—the present job description—and a chance to update and refresh it to meet your company's current needs. Either way, you need to be clear—and pragmatic—about the qualifications.

There is an art to writing job descriptions. According to human resources expert Judith Lindenberger[21] the description should provide a snapshot of the position and needs to clearly and concisely communicate the tasks and responsibilities, along with the qualifications, including the basic requirements, such as specific credentials or skills. She differentiates between tasks ("what the person . . . will actually do"), qualifications ("the skills, attributes, or credentials [needed] to perform each task"), and credentials, such as degrees and licenses.

She outlines the categories that make up an effective job description:

- Title of the position
- Department
- Reports to (to whom the person directly reports)
- Overall responsibility
- Key areas of responsibility
- Consults with (those who the person works with on a regular basis)
- Term of employment
- Qualifications (necessary skills and experience required)

Source: "How to Write a Job Description," Copyright © 2006 The Lindenberger Group, LLC, *www.lindenbergergroup.com*. Used with permission.

Following is a sample job description.

Description: Manager, IT Service Center

The Enterprise IT Service Center is a full-service technical support center that provides immediate assistance for customers and clients. This includes the support of proprietary business applications, EDI and Windows-based business-to-business products and solutions, enterprise resource planning systems, standard desktop applications, and the associated hardware platforms, databases, and network connectivity.

The Manager, Enterprise IT Service Center has responsibility for developing and leading a team of tier 1 support analysts supporting business applications and the requisite processes and programs that support them.

Core Responsibilities Include:
- Provide tactical and strategic direction to a large operational tier one business application support team.
- Understand the EIT Service Delivery Model and associated Service Level Agreements. Manage effectively to agreed-upon levels of service and encourage continuous improvement to processes and associated measurement systems.
- Participate in department strategic planning and process improvement initiatives with EIT leaders and process improvement teams . . . and so forth, listing a total of ten responsibilities.

Knowledge/Skills Requirements:
Balanced technical skills coupled with business and general management competencies.

- Specific experience in the technical service delivery field, preferably with help desk or call center services.

continued

- Relevant professional experience gained over a minimum of five to seven years including some management-level experience.
- Demonstrated results in leading and developing teams, preferably large, operational teams.
- Ability to provide clear direction quickly and on-demand . . . (and so on listing half-dozen more responsibilities).

Physical/Mental Requirements:
- Work is often stressful and occurs with deadlines, limited guidance or information and with large-scale business consequences.
- Frequent shifting of priorities requires great flexibility, solid organizational skills and the mental disposition to shift leadership and focus accordingly.
- Highly results oriented position that requires the need, at times, to put in additional and/or unplanned hours.

Education: BA/BS degree

Work Environment:
- Position is located in a climate-controlled office setting.
- 75 percent of time is spent sitting.
- Out-of-town travel required < 5 percent.

Reports to: Director, IT Service Center
Direct Reports: 2–4
Extended Team: 20–50

(Source: Barbara May. Used with permission.)

Educational and experience requirements represent a gray area. Managers should allow leeway for both, as job experience may qualify an individual with less education who meets specific requirements. However, avoid putting ceilings on experience ("can have no more than twenty years' experience in line assembly") as it may be construed as age discrimination.

Also, be specific in delineating the desired duties. For instance, describe the software programs in which the candidates should be proficient (Word, Excel) instead of merely saying the person needs to be computer literate; that the candidate should to be able to clearly explain and interpret technical information to all types of audiences, rather than having good communications skills, and so forth.

ASK THE RIGHT QUESTIONS

OK, so you've got the job posted, and you've set up interviews. Whether the human resources person has screened the candidates for you or whether you've done it yourself, you're likely faced with a list of prospective employees. So how do you go about interviewing them and picking the best candidate in a fair and equitable manner?

Authors Bob Nelson and Peter Economy[22] recommend taking time to develop a list of questions. After all, if you don't ask the right questions, you won't get the answers you need! Questions should determine why the person is there (hopefully more than because she needs a job; what drew her to your company/job in particular?), what she can do for the company (as opposed to what you can do for her), what kind of person she is (whether she will fit in with the corporate culture and company mission), and whether or not you can come to an agreement on salary. You also need to be familiar with the person's resume, so you can ask questions relating to her particular work history, goals, and educational experience.

The interview should be in a comfortable environment, so all concerned can be as relaxed as possible (although you as a manager may be slightly nervous, consider how the candidate must feel). Putting people in an artificial situation by asking loaded questions or being intimidating will hardly provide a fair assessment of the individual's abilities. However, don't hesitate to ask tough questions about her past experiences, as her responses will often provide a good indication of her strengths and weaknesses. One way to accomplish this is through behavioral interviewing (see below).

Finally, take lots of notes. The human memory is notoriously inaccurate, and a written record will provide an instant refresher course. If someone appears nervous or uneasy when responding to a question or is a particularly impressive candidate, make a note of that as well.

Behavioral Interviewing: A New Wrinkle

Increasingly companies are using what's known as "behavioral interviewing." The premise behind this relatively new method is that past performance can provide the most accurate forecast of future actions. Behavioral interviewing is believed to be over five times more predictive of future on-the-job performance than traditional interviewing.

Although open-ended questions may be asked in both types of interviews, behavioral interviewing takes it a step further by probing the reasons behind specific actions, thus making it more difficult for applicants to "fudge" information or gloss over answers. According to author and human relations expert Katharine Hansen,[23] behavioral interviews evaluate success potential of applicants: "The interviewer identifies job-related experiences, behaviors, knowledge, skills and abilities that the company has decided are desirable in a particular position. The employer then structures very pointed questions to elicit detailed responses aimed at determining if the candidate possesses the desired characteristics." Questions may not even be stated as such and may be phrased like, "Tell me about the time you had to counsel an employee about poor performance" or "Describe a situation in which you had to deal with a production problem."

CAREFULLY EVALUATE YOUR CANDIDATES

Once you've lined up a list of prospective candidates, there's still more work to do. You may be wowed by the good-looking, fast-talking guy or gal, but what if they lied about their qualifications on their resume? And what are they like to work with on a day-to-day basis? And although you may be tempted to dismiss the fashion-impaired, noncommunicative geek, further digging may uncover the fact that the person is in fact a genius in their field (consider the TV show *Monk*).

Following are some steps to help avoid these kinds of disastrous decisions:

Check the candidate's references or designate someone to do this for you. Although checking references can be boring, tedious, and may require persistence in getting in touch with the pertinent people, not only does it verify what the candidate is telling you but it gives you a glimpse of what he may really be like. References can include academic advisors (more people than you might realize actually lie about this!); current and former managers; and colleagues and special interest associations, who may have additional information about the person's reputation and work habits.

But be careful when making inquiries. For example, although you can ask about John's attendance and sales records, avoid questions about his family or ethnic background as such requests for information are considered discriminatory. If you're checking the references with a company (rather than an individual) they likely won't give you much information other than the time period the person worked there and his job title.

Look over all your information. Once you've gathered together everything—job description, interview questions, resumes, notes taken during the interview, and references, it's time to do some sorting. Nelson and Economy[24] recommend designating candidates into the following categories: winners ("clearly the best choices"), potential winners ("questionable for one reason or another," to be hired only after further investigation or if the A-list is unavailable). A third category would be nonwinners (aka "losers" according to Nelson and Economy), those who are clearly unacceptable for the job. Only then will you have all the information to make a decision.

If necessary call them in for a second (or third) interview. Yes, this takes additional time, but sometimes first impressions are incorrect. You can probably think of at least one friend who you didn't particularly like off the bat, but after you got to know him, he turned out to be one of your closest buddies. The same can be true for employees; you'll be spending at least as much (if not more) time with them than many of your friends!

TRUST YOUR GUT

Most hiring and firing decisions are based on objective criteria, the previously mentioned qualifications for hiring; and well-documented information regarding firing to be discussed in the next few sections. However, when everything seems equal—particularly in hiring—sometimes it comes down to "gut" decisions. After looking at all the data (and even maybe listing the positives and negatives of each candidate) you may find someone with a spark of enthusiasm and talent who may have less experience than the other candidates. You find yourself drawn to him for reasons you can't quite define, other than it feels right. That is where your gut instinct comes into play.

Conversely, if you have a bad feeling about someone who is equally qualified, consider that as well. Perhaps he's giving off nonverbal cues that he's not really interested in doing the work or you have a sense that his personality might not mesh well with the team's. Although these things are intangible, they are important. You don't want to be six months down the road, thinking, "I knew I shouldn't have hired so-and-so! Now what am I going to do?"

Make sure to keep in touch with your top candidates. First choices do not always work out, and other positions they qualify for may eventually become available in your company.

PERFORMANCE PROBLEMS VERSUS MISCONDUCT

The section "Employee Discipline—A Call to Improvement" on page 169 discussed the difference between performance problems and misconduct. In general, misconduct is more serious, a willful act on the part of the employee while performance problems usually occur due to lack of or incorrect information or loss of motivation.

Many times performance areas can be corrected through proper training and coaching, starting with *verbal counseling*, the first step in dealing with such issues. Verbal counseling can range from a casual encounter in the hallway ("Louise, you forgot to send me the sales documentation sheet. Please do so the next time.") to a sit-down meeting, where you discuss specific problem areas and focus on issues needing correction. Verbal counseling is rarely documented in the employee's file, unless he continues to make the same mistake and you need to take further action.

That next step is *written counseling*, a more formal session with the manager that usually involves a memo and other documentation of the discussion as to how the problems will be remedied. At this point, you can draw up a plan of improvement for the team member that explicitly states the goals, the schedule for attainment, and the training necessary to achieve those goals. You may also need to point out the potential consequences should the person fail to improve, whether it be a reassignment to a less challenging position, a formal record of the problem to be placed in the person's file, or in some instances, loss of pay.[25]

If these measures fail to do the trick, you may have to consider the progressively more serious sanctions discussed in the next section.

GET IT IN WRITING—KEEPING IT LEGAL

Although each company has different disciplinary procedures—and you, as a manager, should be familiar with them, and know where to get additional information should you have any questions—what follows is a basic description of the progressive disciplinary actions.

Reprimands are used with repeated incidences of misconduct and less often with performance problems. They can be written or oral, although they are almost always documented. Reprimands also generally go into the employee's file and are passed along to higher levels of the organization. Also known as a written warning, a reprimand is often the last stop before the more serious steps are taken.

Probation. Normally probation applies only to new hires, who are put on a probation period of anywhere from thirty days to six months. The new hire can be terminated anytime during the probationary period if he fails to perform or is otherwise deemed unsuitable to work for the company. If he performs well, the probationary status is removed.

Some companies, however, use probationary status for employees whose work has fallen below standards or for reasons of misconduct. In these cases, they are given a set period of time to shape up or ship out, to improve/change their work/behavior, or, they are warned, more severe measures will be taken.

Demotion/Reassignment. This involves placing the individual in a different or lower position within the organization. Sometimes he receives a cut in salary, although it's better for his morale and performance to receive at least equivalent pay (he may not, however, get the raise or promotion promised with his previous job). Generally speaking, demotions/reassignments are due to performance issues, rather than misconduct. Sometimes they are for the best: Employees can be hired/promoted to certain positions only to find out they can't handle the duties and responsibilities. If such is the case, help them see the "glass half full" aspect of the situation; the new job will hopefully be much more suited to their abilities, temperament, and talent.

Suspension. This is leave without pay due to extremely serious misconduct (usually involving blowing up cars/buildings in pursuit of bad guys who are out of the officer's jurisdiction). In business, however, there are disciplinary and nondisciplinary suspensions. With the former, just about every other avenue has been exhausted, and the employee must be removed from the workplace for a set period of time, for purposes of safety or to help restore team morale. If it's nondisciplinary, the employee is put on leave for an indefinite period, while he is being investigated for criminal or other charges. Whether or not the individual is paid during this period is up to company policy.

The final step of course is termination, which will be discussed in the next section.

FIRING: A MANAGER'S TOUGHEST DECISION

This is where the going gets really tough. Doing the paperwork and following procedures are only part of the challenge. The rest lies with you, the manager, and the employee you need to let go. If you're lucky they'll "fire" themselves and quit, leaving you with the comparatively minor headache of finding a replacement, if one is needed.

Sometimes the basis for termination has little to do with the employee at all; the company is simply conducting layoffs, and your team member is slated to go. Or the company is reorganizing, and certain jobs have been eliminated. Often these kinds of lay-offs are done in clusters—that is, more than one person is removed at the same time—so that makes it a less bitter pill to swallow and the team members usually qualify for unemployment and/or severance benefits.

Much harder to handle are the situations where someone is being fired because every avenue has been tried—and exhausted—to improve his performance or behavior. The job itself may have evolved, and the person is unable to adapt. Or the employee has committed an act of misconduct—such as sexual harassment or drug use—and the only choice is to let them go.

However, even firings can be handled with grace and aplomb. Author and management expert Malcolm Tatum[26] recommends using a place that's private, such as a conference room. Only those who are directly involved—managerial personnel, wit-nesses—should be told in advance and, if necessary, be present. Having a third party in the room is usually a good idea, "someone who understands the gravity of the situation and who will hold the discussion and details of the termination to be confidential in nature."

He also recommends that managers avoid using sweeping statements and being specific, citing this example: "Joe, you have missed your weekly sales quota every week for the last three months. The phone logs show you did not make your minimum number of sales calls on any day within those three months. Your performance is not acceptable." Additionally:

- Stick to the facts and subjects related to the termination—final pay, expense reports, health insurance, retirement accounts, and other related issues.
- If severance is being offered include details on that as well.
- Firings should be done late in the day so as not to disrupt the workplace. Depending upon company policy and/or the situa-tion, the employee may or may not be allowed to clean out his desk at the time (with the assistance of a trusted staff member

so no company property is removed). Sometimes, his personal effects are mailed to him.

- The manager is responsible for safeguarding company property including customer contact information. For this reason, sales people are generally escorted immediately from the premises and personal effects are sent to them. Generally speaking, their e-mail and system access are also immediately revoked within minutes as people sometimes send angry e-mails to a company-wide distribution list.
- Be sympathetic but firm, and under no circumstances show any indication that you're unsure or thinking about changing your mind. Stay away from rehashing past performance or promises to improve. At this point, all chances for saving their job are gone.
- Termination is an emotional situation, and the team member may not hear what you've said the first time, so you may have to repeat yourself to make sure he's understood everything. Also give him the information in writing, and if he becomes angry or abusive, stay calm (make sure that Security is nearby just in case). Remember, he is leaving, not you, and he is naturally quite upset.

Few if any managers look forward to firing employees. But keeping things on a courteous and professional level will help make it less painful for everyone.

TAKE-AWAY POINTS

- Job descriptions are important and provide a "snapshot" of the position. Make sure to include accurate and realistic tasks, qualifications, and credentials.
- During an interview, put candidates at ease and ask pointed, specific questions. Take notes to refresh your memory for when you review all applicants.

- Take time to evaluate all applicants carefully, paying close attention to their qualifications and work ethic rather than surface charm and looks.
- Sometimes hiring someone comes down to gut instinct. When that's the case, make sure decisions are based in fact. But when all else is equal, it's a good idea to follow your instincts, as you don't want to end up firing the person a few months later.
- Performance problems are different from misconduct and should be dealt with accordingly. However, if, after repeated conversations and attempts to correct, no change is forthcoming, you'll need to document everything and may have to progress to other disciplinary levels.
- When disciplining a team member, make sure you're familiar with the company's disciplinary procedures and follow them to the letter.
- If you must fire someone, have all documents in order and be as objective and calm as possible. Try to keep the situation on a professional level at all times.

CHAPTER 14

Effective Appraisals

CHAPTER OBJECTIVES

To understand the purpose of an appraisal or regular review

To learn why appraisals are important

To grasp some principles to help you prepare for and run effective appraisals or regular reviews

INTRODUCTION

An organization's objectives are achieved by the successful accomplishment of individual goals. To do this, people require feedback and help. The manager also needs the opportunity to communicate and clarify the direction of the department and the standards required. Hence the need for performance appraisals.

Some organizations use the term *appraisal*, while others prefer *performance review*, to refer to a regular meeting where the manager and team member formally discuss the team member's performance and set objectives for the coming period. This is usually a three-, six-, or twelve-month period since the last formal discussion. Most companies today have some sort of appraisal system. If yours does not, perhaps this chapter will provide some ideas for implementing one.

DEFINITION AND PURPOSE OF APPRAISALS

An *appraisal or regular review* is a formal—that is, one in which key points are noted in writing—and regularly scheduled discussion between the manager and team member to jointly:

- Review the team member's performance over the period since the last appraisal/review.
- Discuss her training needs in her current role and appropriate actions.
- Agree on her performance objectives for the coming period.

Some appraisal or review meetings also cover career development needs and actions, although sometimes this aspect is discussed separately. In many companies, performance appraisals are conducted in conjunction with yearly salary discussions. Also many companies separate the performance appraisal for the previous/current year from the objective-setting discussion for the next year.

The benefits to the *manager* include:

* Performance improvement (reinforcing strengths and addressing areas for improvement)
* Justification for salary treatment, if applicable
* Motivation via objective feedback
* Specific assessment of the team member's training needs in their current role
* If applicable, identifying future career potential and addressing development needs

The benefits for the *team member* are:

* Providing the answer to "How am I doing?"
* Personal involvement in training plans (and, if applicable, career development plans)
* A positive outcome due to reinforcement of strengths and a constructive approach to dealing with areas for improvement

PROVIDE REGULAR FEEDBACK AT OTHER TIMES

Following is a scenario that often occurs during appraisals.

Manager: "Over the last year, on ten out of twelve occasions, you were two weeks late with your monthly reports. That caused me serious problems, Mandy, as I had to guess at the figures for my summary report."

Mandy: "Sorry, but to be honest, I thought they were forms that everyone has to complete but nothing is actually done with them."

Manager: "Well, if you saw the grief I got from our director, you would view them differently. They must be in on time in the future—and make sure you do it without me having to remind you!"

Mandy: "Hold on a minute, Peter. Why on earth didn't you tell me all this ten months ago? Why let it go this long?"

Unfortunately, some managers only discuss performance difficulties during the appraisal. By then, it is usually too late to do anything useful (as in the above example). This leaves the team member feeling as if she's been unfairly chastised, not to mention upset by the fact that her manager failed to communicate with her about a problem. She may wonder what else she's done to upset the manager that the manager isn't telling her about.

Avoid surprises by regularly reviewing performance during the year. The section "Meet with Team Members Regularly" on page 168 recommends meeting with staff members on a monthly basis. Thus, in the example above, Peter would have discussed the late reports with Mandy when the problem first appeared. This action would have avoided nine recurrences of the problem—and an unpleasant surprise during the appraisal!

JOINTLY AGREE ON PERFORMANCE OBJECTIVES

Some managers believe their role in the appraisal or review is to adopt a commanding stance and tell the team member what is expected of her in the coming year. They also see setting performance objectives as a strictly managerial task. In this scenario, the team member has little if any chance for comment or disagreement. Such an approach might reduce any dissention or argumentative discussion, but is the team member committed to those objectives? Most people resent being told what to do and react accordingly.

While some performance objectives are easily measured (for example, sales revenue, number of computer programs written, and so on), others are less easy to define without discussion (for example, cooperation within the team, providing advice to other departments, and so forth). The manager's criteria for cooperation, for instance, may be markedly different from that of the team member. Without discussion, the manager might set a target seen as unreasonable or even inappropriate by the team member.

The best method—and way to elicit cooperation—is to come to a mutual consensus on performance objectives. Encourage team members to produce their list of suggested objectives before the discussion. During the appraisal, compare it with your own list. You will probably find that you both agree on perhaps 80 percent, which only leaves 20 percent to be resolved.

For hard-to-measure objectives—for example, cooperation—define what indicates that cooperation is taking place. For instance, you might both believe that it means taking the initiative for helping others in a crisis. In this way, both manager and team member know what is expected and how cooperation can be judged.

FIND A USEFUL RATING SCALE

Rating scales that evaluate standards using words such as "excellent," "good," "fair," or "poor" can cause serious problems and fail to clearly delineate what is meant. One person's definition of "good" is not the same as another's. For example, is a "good" meal while dining out cheap, tasty, high-class, served promptly, or allowing everyone to take their time, all of these, none of these, or what? Suppose the team member feels she has delivered a "good" performance and the manager would only rate it as "fair." As you can see, there is a clear disconnect on a point that is very difficult to quantify.

Also, some managers are tougher (or softer) than others: "I never give 'excellent.' Nobody is that good!" or "I will give all my people 'good' to keep them motivated." None of these observations is objective, and people expect (and want) accurate feedback on their performance.

Whatever rating scale you use, make sure it is *clearly defined*. That way both the individual and manager know precisely what's being talked about. For example:

1. Performs consistently above expected level of performance (with the "level of performance" being, for example, X dollars in sales per month, or equipment being repaired within X amount of time).
2. Performs occasionally above expected level of performance.
3. Achieves expected level of performance.
4. Performs below expected level of performance.

As mentioned previously "expected level of performance" has been clearly defined, so both manager and team member know the specific areas to be addressed as well as those where the team member has excelled. A helpful tool is James E. Neal Jr.'s book *Effective Phrases for Performance Appraisals* 10th ed. (G. Neil, 2003) which offers thousands of quantifiable phrases describing the key performance factors.

ALLOW SUFFICIENT TIME FOR THE APPRAISAL

Some managers view the appraisal or review as another annoying "personnel form" to be filled in and filed away as quickly as possible. However, they are doing themselves and their team members a great disservice by only allowing a short time for the appraisal and/or only giving it cursory thought. A tool to help the organization reach its goals, a properly used appraisal will greatly help all concerned.

The appraisal discussion should, at the very least, cover performance over the preceding period and objectives for the coming period. An effective appraisal or review requires the active involvement of both the manager and team member. It therefore takes a fair amount of time to be carried out properly. That time investment is more than worth it in terms of performance benefits and future motivation.

So what is a "reasonable amount of time"? As a rule of thumb, estimate how long you think the appraisal or review discussion will take, and then double it! Often, an effective discussion takes more than an hour and a half. But which is more useful: ninety minutes of joint discussion in which the staff member truly understands her performance and feels a sense of "ownership" in doing the job properly, or twenty minutes in which the manager tells the person what she's doing wrong, resulting in a lack of insight and a possible loss of motivation?

HOW DO *THEY* THINK THEY HAVE DONE?

Managers sometimes feel they need to be both judge and jury regarding the team member's performance. For instance, an evaluation of someone who does training might go like this: "Well, Karl, you have performed extremely well with regard to the courses you have run, but you should make more use of the computer in presentations. That needs to improve for next year. Okay?"

As mentioned earlier, telling someone they have a particular strength or weakness does not mean that they will necessarily believe you! What if Karl replied: "No, Marion, that's not really fair. I investigated the use of computers five months ago and decided they were of little benefit with the type of training I do. I even mentioned it to you at the time."

Moreover, this "feedback" is vague. What in particular has Karl done well when teaching courses and how, specifically, might he make better use of the computer?

Before the appraisal or review, ask the team member to consider the following:

- What have they done well, and why?
- What could they improve, and how?

During the discussion, you can compare your views and will likely find that your perceptions are fairly close to theirs in many areas. Agreement on these points is therefore easy. The time can then be spent discussing any areas where you differ and exploring the "whys" and "hows."

SPEND MOST OF THE TIME LOOKING FORWARD

Let's say an appraisal or review takes place in December 2007, covering performance during 2007 and objectives for 2008. How much time should be spent looking at performance in 2007 as compared with examining objectives for 2008? Many managers think that 70 to 80 percent of the time should be spent reviewing past performance, with 20 to 30 percent looking forward. This is because:

1. Managers must review the entire year because few (or no) discussions have taken place during that period.
2. It is easier to talk about what occurred in the past rather than what should happen in the future.

However, the performance appraisal would be more effective if you reversed the percentages—that is, spending 20 percent of the time looking backward and 80 percent looking forward. You can't change the past—it's gone—you can only learn from it. You can look to the future to encourage change for the better. Therefore:

- Review performance regularly throughout the period. The appraisal or review discussion then only needs to involve a summary of what has already been talked about. Discuss the team member's career goals and interests and provide guidance as to how to achieve them.

- Encourage the team member to prepare for the appraisal or review discussion by thinking about how well they performed in the current year along with how they can improve and what their goals are for the next year.

AGREE ON JOINT ACTION PLANS

Most appraisal or review systems call for action plans and refer to the need for these plans to be jointly agreed upon. However, some managers take the view that the only person who is supposed to take any action is the team member. They see no need for action or contribution on their own part.

Although many actions should be jointly agreed upon to ensure "commitment," most team members need some help from their boss to make things happen. Many times managers will say something like, "We have agreed that you need to learn about running departmental meetings. So how do you think *you* might obtain that information?" This puts the onus entirely on the team member and leaves them hanging without a sense of support from the manager. They may feel at a loss as to how to go about doing this.

A better way to phrase the question might be: "We have agreed that you need to learn about running departmental meetings. So how do you think *we* can best accomplish this?" Knowing that you're there for the team member might spark some specific ideas from them, such as additional study of the topic or attending a seminar. You might offer to let the employee run one of your meetings and give them feedback afterward. Joint action plans should be an agreed-on series of measures involving *both* the manager and the team member, rather than leaving the team member completely on their own.

BUILD UPON AND PUT JOINT ACTION PLANS INTO "ACTION"

It's one thing to produce a joint action plan, but what happens to it after the appraisal is completed? Unfortunately, some first-rate action plans are unceremoniously buried under "Appraisal" in the employee's file, to be resurrected only at the next appraisal/review. At that stage, some time will be spent bemoaning the fact that certain things should have happened: "Oh dear, I was supposed to arrange a computer course for you, wasn't I?"

In order to make the action plan a living document, managers should do the following:

1. Give the team member a copy of the action plan and ask them to note specific dates, etc., in their diary.
2. Make a copy of each action plan (the original stays with the appraisal or review documentation) and place it where you can easily access it. Make a note on your calendar (either electronic or paper) to serve as a reminder that the action must be taken at the planned time.

If you have adopted monthly meetings with your team, consider reviewing progress on the action plan at those meetings.

APPRAISING YOURSELF AS A MANAGER

Ask yourself how you feel about the prospect of telling your manager what they do well and how they could improve your working relationship. Your enthusiasm for this idea likely depends upon how well you get along with your current manager.

Then ask yourself how your team members would react if you invited them to appraise you. Often the most effective managers encourage feedback from their team, while those who actually need it rarely, if ever, ask for it. Some fear they might stir up a hornet's nest of dissention (they well might!) while others believe they would lose respect if they allowed criticism, not realizing that taking notice of constructive comments increases respect.

However, getting team members to provide constructive feedback is a vital part of being an effective manager. Not only does it indicate a high opinion of your leadership but it encourages team ownership of responsibilities and open communication.

So from time to time, consider asking team members whose opinions you respect the following, with an eye to improving the way you work together.

* What do you think I, as your manager, do well and why?
* What do you think I, as your manager, could improve and how?
* What actions should we take?

You may also get negative feedback from a team member whose opinion you may not value as highly. However, take what he says under serious consideration as well. Even though you may not always agree with his views, they may be justified in this case.

By talking (and listening) to all of your team members, you can get a fairly good idea of how you're functioning as a manager. Aim to encourage balanced, useful (constructive) feedback, and listen!

TAKE-AWAY POINTS

* Avoid surprises by allowing regular feedback during the appraisal/review period.
* Jointly agree on performance objectives for the coming period.
* Make sure the rating scale matches the job requirements and is specific.
* Allow plenty of time for appraisals so you can work together on solutions with the team member.

- Ask team members how well they've done and have them suggests ways they think they can improve. Work on those areas in which you disagree.
- Spend most of the time looking at matters that need improvement in the future, rather than at past mistakes or problems.
- Make sure joint action plans are a collaborative effort between you and the team member and be responsible for and schedule their implementation.
- As a manager, you need "appraisal" as well, so encourage feedback and listen to it carefully.

Conclusion

This book covered new and basic concepts to help with a wide range of management activities. Whether you have read the entire book or selected chapters that were of relevance, I hope you've gained useful ideas and information.

However, it's only a beginning; many of the books, articles, and Web sites referenced in the endnotes will provide even more information, and threads that will lead to further knowledge. Learning about management, or anything for that matter, is best considered an ongoing process: My father, an optometrist, graduated from college in the 1930s and continued to attend various seminars and classes until his death in 1991.

Given the vast amount of information, concepts, and opinions on the subject of business and management, it may be difficult to separate the "wheat from the chaff," so to speak, at least initially. Here is where your network of friends, colleagues, and even mentors (managers can have mentors too!) can be especially useful in sorting out information and providing useful leads and suggestions. Don't hesitate to ask for their help.

Finally, remember the 80:20 rule as you move into your management role. Decide which ideas will be of most significant use to you now, and then determine how and when you will implement them.

Regardless of whom you manage or where you're employed, some basics remain the same. With knowledge, hard work, and a "little help from your friends" (like this book) you can adapt and become effective as both a manager and contributor, leading your team and company to whatever goals you aspire.

Endnotes

1. Warner, Bill. "Talking Management: What Is a Manager, and What Does He or She Really Do?" online article Local Tech Wire, 4 Dec. 2005 (*www.localtechwire.com/business/local_tech_wire/opinion/story/11629660*)

2. Schein, Edgar. *Organizational Culture and Leadership*, 3rd ed. (San Francisco: Jossey-Bass, 2004)

3. Deal, Terrence E. and Allan A. Kennedy. *Corporate Cultures* (New York: Perseus, 2000)

4. McGregor, Douglas. *The Human Side of Enterprise*, rev. ed. (New York: McGraw-Hill, 2006)

5. Crittendon, Robert. *The New Manager's Starter Kit* (New York: Amacom, 2002), 16

6. Covi, Ida. "Leading the Workplace Within" online article Business Know How, nd (*www.businessknowhow.com/manage/leadwithin.htm*)

7. "Managing a Multicultural Workforce," online article WorldRoom (*www.worldroom.com/pages/career/mtoolbox03200305.phtml*)

8. "Ten Tips for Managing Creative Types," online article, All Business, nd (*www.allbusiness.com/human-resources/workforce-management/2975119-1.html*)

9. Cochran, Sarah. "Worker's Compensation: An Overview," Wex: The Legal Information Institute, Cornell University Law School, 18 June 2007. (*www.law.cornell.edu/wex/index.php/Workers_compensation#workers.27_compensation:_an_overview*)

10. *Roget's New Millennium™ Thesaurus, First Edition.* Thesaurus.com Web site. Lexico Publishing Group, 2007 (*thesaurus.reference.com/browse/problem*)

11. Ruiz, Don Miguel. *The Four Agreements* (San Rafael, CA: Amber-Allen, 1997), 63–74

12. "Creativity at Work." Ozone Web site. London, 2006 (*www.odysseyzone.com/Articles/Creativityatwork/tabid/99/Default.aspx*)

13. Moi, Ali, et al. *Managing for Excellence* (New York: DK, 2001), 222–7

14. Covey, Stephen R. *The Seven Habits of Highly Effective People* (New York: Free Press, 2004)

15. Agnew, Beth. "Benefits and Pitfalls of Coaching Employees," paper, nd. Seneca College of Applied Arts & Technology (*www.wetherhaven.com/~conversation/Documents/coaching-benefits-pitfalls.pdf*)

16. "Coaching and Mentoring" online article, Impact Factory Web site, nd. (*www.impactfactory.com/gate/coaching_mentoring_skills_training/freegate_1825-1104-1118.html*)

17. *Managing for Excellence*, 223

18. "Lead: Mentoring" online article, Small Business Administration, nd (*www.sba.gov/smallbusinessplanner/manage/lead/SERV_MENTORING.html*)

19. "Planning a Retreat," online article, Adventure Associates, nd. (*www.adventureassoc.com/services/corporate-retreats.html*)

20. Nelson, Bob and Peter Economy. *Managing for Dummies* (New York: Wiley, 2003), 232–33

21. Lindenberger, Judith. "How to Write a Job Description," online article Business Know How, nd. (*www.businessknowhow.com/manage/jobdesc.htm*)

22. *Managing for Dummies*, 65–67

23. Hansen, Katharine. "Behavioral Interviewing Strategies," online article Quintessential Careers (*www.quintcareers.com/behavioral_interviewing.html*)

24. *Managing for Dummies*, 72

25. Ibid., 237, 241

26. Tatum, Malcolm. "How to Fire Employees," online article How to Do Things, 8 June 2006 (*www.howtodothings.com/business/a3074-how-to-fire-employees.html*)s

Index

About the Authors

Sandra Gurvis has been a freelance writer for more than thirty years. The author of eleven books, she has written corporate profiles and technical articles for clients such as The Ohio State University Medical Center, Merrill Lynch, Quantum Tapes, and Battelle Memorial Institute, and has written for publications including *Selling Power, Creativity, ASRT Scanner, Optical Technology, The World & I*, and *Spirit* magazine. A member of the American Society of Journalists and Authors and the American Medical Writers Association, Sandra has won many awards for her writing, Additionally, she has created Web content for AOL CityGuide, homestore.com, worth.com, and others.

Her titles include *Day Trips From Columbus* (2004); *Careers for Nonconformists* (2000), which was a selection of the Quality Paperback Book Club; *The Well-Traveled Dog* (2001); *America's Strangest Museums* (1998); and more. Her books have been featured on *Good Morning America, CBS Up to the Minute*, and *ABC World News Tonight* and other radio and TV stations nationwide, in *USA Today* and other newspapers, and they have been excerpted in magazines. Her newest title is *Ohio Curiosities* (2007).

A major aspect of her work has been on the Vietnam protests and their aftereffects. Particularly relevant to today's political situation is her recent nonfiction title, *Where Have All the Flower Children Gone?* (2006). It covers all facets of the Vietnam era, from tracking the student protest and conservative movements to comparing the controversy surrounding Vietnam to the Middle East. Her novel, *The Pipe Dreamers* (2001), is a fictional exploration of the late 1960s and early 1970s, mostly set in the small college town of Hampton, Ohio. She has also written on this topic for the *VVA Veteran, Ohio State Alumni Magazine, People*, and other publications. More information about Sandra and her books can be found on *www.sgurvis.com* and *www.booksaboutthe60s.com*. She lives in Columbus, OH.

Barbara J. May has successfully managed up to 300 employees in order-processing and customer-care organizations. She currently works for Qwest Communications as the manager of sales operations, where she is responsible for a staff of 150 management employees. She received her bachelor of science in business administration from The Ohio State University and is a certified continuous process improvement facilitator. She lives in Hilliard, OH.